THE

ABUNDANT

LIFE

"I have come that they may have life, and that they may have it more abundantly."

John 10:10

Greg E. Viehman, M.D.

Author:	Greg E. Viehman, M.D.
Editor:	Greg McElveen
Reviewers:	DeeAnn Williamson / Leslie Williamson
Cover Illustration, design © 2015	Marketing Ministries
Cover Photo © 2015	Shutterstock.com
Interior photos © 2015	Shutterstock.com

Library of Congress Control Number:

1. BS2525-2544 Study and teaching
2. BT750-811 Salvation. Soteriology
3. BT1095-1255 Apologetics. Evidences of Christianity
4. BV205-287 Prayer
5. BV4625-4627 Sins and vices

BISAC / Classification Suggestions:

1. REL006700 RELIGION / Biblical Studies / Bible Study Guides
2. REL012000 RELIGION / Christian Life / General
3. REL012070 RELIGION / Christian Life / Personal Growth
4. REL012120 RELIGION / Christian Life / Spiritual Growth
5. REL099000 RELIGION / Christian Life / Spiritual Warfare

ISBN-13: 978-1-937355-22-7 V 1.0

TABLE OF CONTENTS

INTRODUCTION   6

THE ABUNDANT LIFE PATHWAY   12

OUTLINE   14

PART I   ABUNDANT REVELATION   15

WEEK 1   Abundant Need, Provision, Salvation Evaluation   16

WEEK 2   Abundant Change, Newness, Worth   36

WEEK 3   Abundant Wealth, Power, Freedom   56

WEEK 4   Abundant Security, Hope, Plans   76

PART II   ABUNDANT RESPONSE   95

WEEK 5   Abundant Surrender, Praise, Words   96

WEEK 6   Abundant God, Repentance, Love for God, Health   114

HEART EVALUATION   140

PART III   ABUNDANT HEALTH   143

WEEK 7   Abundant Growth, Godliness   146

WEEK 8   Abundant Struggle, Suffering, Victory   160

WEEK 9   Abundant Love for Others, Giving   178

WEEK 10   Abundant Service, Harvest   190

ACKNOWLEDGEMENTS

This project began when I was reading *John 10:10*. Jesus said that He had come for us to have "abundant life." At that moment the LORD put it on my heart to study this verse and to learn what it means for Christians today. I began with a word study on "abundant," and from there it took on a life of its own that was completely guided by God. He showed me the pathway for anyone to live the abundant life that He gave His life for. I thank the LORD who is the true author of my life and the inspiration behind this study. God has enabled me to do something not possible without Him

I am very grateful to many people who God used to help me complete this study guide. Their contributions, time, and insights have been invaluable. Bill Vanarthos, M.D., Bill Dunn, Archie Murray, Aaron Lee, and Greg Hales served as editors. Leslie and DeeAnn Williamson, Sarah Land, and Kathy Phipps were stellar editors for content, punctuation, and grammar. Marketing Ministries did an outstanding job for creative design and layout. Jason Faber was project manager and John Sierra the senior designer. Greg McElveen's role as an editor and publisher was invaluable and essential to the project. Also, many people contributed their comments and ideas before the final version was written. I thank them for their time, interest, and contributions. Finally, my wife Ruth has given me the time, encouragement, and strength to spend the countless hours needed over the past two years.

Greg E. Viehman, M.D.

ABOUT THE AUTHOR

Dr. Viehman was born and raised in Wilmington, Delaware. He graduated magna cum laude from the University of Delaware. Dr. Viehman attended medical school at Jefferson Medical College in Philadelphia, Pennsylvania and graduated number one in his class. He completed an Internship in Internal Medicine at the Hospital of the University of Pennsylvania in Philadelphia, and a dermatology residency at Duke University Medical Center, where he was chief resident. Dr. Viehman completed his fellowship in skin cancer surgery also at Duke. Dr. Viehman cofounded the Cary Skin Center in Cary, North Carolina, and worked there 1998-2008. He is now in solo private practice at SeaCoast Skin Surgery in Wilmington, NC.

Dr. Viehman has lectured nationally on dermatologic surgery and authored several published scientific research articles. He has multiple interests, including, surfing, paddle boarding, swimming, and collecting rare Bibles. Dr. Viehman lives with his wife and three children.

Dr. Viehman is currently completing his masters degree in Theology from Liberty University Baptist Theological Seminary. Dr. Viehman is also the author of "The God Diagnosis: A Physician's Shocking Journey To Life After Death." The book is available online at Amazon.com and other online retailers. He is available for speaking engagements at churches, retreats, schools, Bible studies, and other venues.

See videos & more under resources at abundantlifestudy.com

Visit his ministry web site for more information: everlastingstrength.org.

INTRODUCTION

Do you struggle with sin and defeat on a regular basis? Do you question whether your relationship with God is growing and maturing like it should be? Do you feel defeated and ineffective in your Christian life? Do you wonder where the joy and peace are? Do you suffer from a lack of zeal and genuine desire to serve God and know Him? Have Bible study, devotions, and church become obligation versus opportunity? Maybe you have been a Christian since childhood and wonder why some new Christians saved later in life are so much more excited than you are. Do you sometimes doubt your own salvation? Do you sometimes feel as if you are not saved at all? Or, maybe you are a new Christian and don't want to experience these things.

You do not have to experience an uncertain, defeated, and lackluster Christian life! God wants you to have a life overflowing with joy, meaning, purpose, and zeal for Him. Pastors and Christian writers exhort us to serve God and to fully commit and devote ourselves to Him, but how do we get there? We agree as we listen but then rarely follow through. Why?! The answer to these questions and more will be revealed as you delve into this study guide, The Abundant Life.

In *John 10:10* Jesus said, "I have come that they may have life, and that they may have it more abundantly." What did Jesus mean? What is the abundant life that God wants His children to have? How do we experience the abundant life that Jesus came to provide? This study will examine the abundant life according to Scripture. It is written for Christians who are seeking to live the abundant life and escape a life of defeat. It is designed to help Christians know what the abundant life is and to explain how to practically experience it.

Part I
Abundant Revelation: →
Grace

Part II
Abundant Response: →
Relationship

Part III
Abundant Results:
Transformation/Fruit

The study is divided into three parts that are sequential and interdependent: Part I examines the abundant revelation that God has provided with particular attention to His grace. Grace is unmerited, undeserved, and unearned favor from God which also includes divine enablement to live the Christian life and to do so abundantly. This is beautifully revealed through the life of Jesus Christ and what He accomplished on the cross.

I have talked with many Christians who do not seem to fully comprehend or are simply unaware of God's incredible outpouring of love, mercy, and spiritual blessings which come from salvation. The blessings that come from simply being a child of God are revealed in His Word, and these are profound. So why aren't these benefits known to Christians? Sadly, many pastors and Christian leaders will tell you that many Christians are not reading His Word on a regular basis. From my research and in my opinion, the Gospel of salvation through Jesus Christ emanating from the grace, love, and mercy of God is the most essential element for the Christian life. God's grace gives us what we do not deserve: forgiveness and salvation. God's mercy provides a way to avoid what we do deserve: eternal death and separation from Him in hell.

A proper understanding of God's abundant grace is the fuel and the impetus that leads to Part II of the study: Abundant Response. A response is key! Christianity is not just a ticket to Heaven but to a real relationship with God. An in-depth understanding of the free gift of salvation that Jesus provided to us creates within us a desire to continually respond to God from gratitude. A true relationship is always a two-way street, and our relationship with God should be no different.

Gratitude is a powerful motive for serving God and continually surrendering to Him because it comes from a heart that is in awe and wonder of the grace received through Jesus Christ. I believe that a major problem in Christianity today is that many Christians are unaware of just how much God has done for them and who they are in Christ. They may have been coaxed and "guilted" into serving God without having first been educated on what God has already done for them, and as a result, their response may be one of resentment instead of gratefulness. Once a person truly digests and understands the grace received, as discussed in Part I of this study, he or she cannot help but respond to God from a heart that is eager and willing to serve God and submit to Him from gratitude. The abundant revelation of the grace of God (Part I) causes an abundant response from the Christian to God (Part II).

See videos & more under resources at abundantlifestudy.com

This is exactly why the Gospel is essential for the daily life of the Christian. The Gospel of salvation is not just for the unsaved but is essential for every Christian to meditate on daily. It is the fuel and spark for our response to God. No one will have to ask us to serve and know God when we meditate on where we were before salvation and what God did to save us. No! We will run to Him eagerly, willingly, and expectantly!

When we respond to God's abundant grace, He responds even stronger to us. We respond again and this cycle keeps going! Our response begins with praise, surrender, prayer, and love for God. When we sin and mess up, which we will, we then respond with repentance and gratitude for God's forgiveness and grace in Christ. A stumbling block to the abundant life can be the issue that we all continue to sin and make mistakes even after being saved for many years. Remembering that God has forgiven all our sins—past, present, and future—provides the proper response and perspective when we do sin. The response is not "I continue to sin, so am I really saved?" but "I continue to sin, and I thank you, Jesus, that I am saved and forgiven! Help me to not do that again." This abundant interactive response between a Christian and God is the start of an abundant relationship with Him. This is also a state of spiritual health that will allow the believer to grow and mature in their relationship with the Lord leading to abundant results (Part III).

It is critical to understand that the results come from a healthy heart. Abundant results are a natural result of a healthy heart and relationship with God. The relationship is fueled and maintained by love and gratitude, which come from an understanding of the grace that is received at salvation and that is ongoing every day. The abundant relationship causes abundant transformation and fruit in the Christian's life. Notice that the impetus for the entire process is the Word of God. Each step is a natural result of the prior. They are sequential and interdependent.

We all want results but we cannot have results without health and we cannot have health without relationship. Our starting point should be studying the Scriptures and exploring our relationship of surrender to the Lord. If we are in a right and healthy relationship with the Lord, then the results will follow naturally. We cannot expect results without putting in the time. This is not a Band-Aid or pill, but the effort required is worth it exponentially. This extra effort is motivated by Biblical knowledge, because once we learn God's abundant revelation we cannot wait to get to know Him and study His Word more. One of the major goals we can now address is victory over sin. We will never be sinless but we should sin less and less. All of these blessings combined constitute the abundant life. It can be defined as follows:

The abundant Christian life is a healthy and maturing relationship with the Lord Jesus Christ that is founded upon and maintained by the grace of God. It results in a fruitful life of love for God and others while being continually transformed into the likeness of Christ, which results in gradual victory over sin.

This study has 27 lessons. Each lesson has Bible verses to look up and questions to ponder. The Bible verses are the specific Scriptures that pertain to what is being discussed. For each of these verses, please read the entire paragraph in which it is found to get the context of what is being taught. You may need to read the entire chapter. Please do not just read the verse itself in isolation. The verses are listed to pinpoint the key idea in that part of the Scriptures. Read each of them several times and meditate on them. If a verse is listed several times in a lesson, read it every time it is listed. Many verses teach more than one point at a time, and it is always useful to review.

This study is designed to get you into the Word of God on your own. God's Word is living and powerful! Get everything out of it that He wants you to. The key verses to look up appear first. There are also additional verses after these that are in parentheses for those who want to dig deeper and look up more verses. These are optional. Below is an example:

John 14:2; Luke 13:8; Ephesians 2:1-2 (John 16:10; Romans 10:1-3; Jeremiah 31:3)

Pray and ask for the Holy Spirit to reveal to you what God is saying. Ask God to work in your heart when you read and study. Just looking up the verses and intellectually understanding what God has done does not guarantee the abundant life. Many people know a lot of Scripture and are not living the abundant life. We must pray and allow what we learn to change us by the power of God. We must apply the meaning in the text to our lives and let it change us by submitting to the Holy Spirit.

This study is only intended to be a brief overview of the abundant life. Many of the topics and truths we will study could be the subject of their own study.

See videos & more under resources at abundantlifestudy.com

A deeper study of these various truths can only enhance our ability to live a truly abundant life. The abundant life requires hard work and perseverance, but it is worth it! The study can be performed at your own pace. I have also provided a suggested breakdown of the lessons for weekly group study.

The study also has 16 videos which are essential to watch. Visit www. abundantlifestudy.com to view them online. These videos provide additional information and insight into each week's lessons.

A Leader's Guide is also available on the web site for download. This is designed to assist leaders using The Abundant Life in a group setting.

The word for "abundant" in the Greek means a superfluous overflow or excess that is exceedingly beyond measure and beyond what is necessary. It means something that is superior in quantity and quality. This is exciting! Clearly, God wants us to have an amazing life that abounds here on earth. We do not have to be joyless Christians going through the motions anymore! We can have victory over sin and know the God who created us and saved us. Let's get going and discover the abundant life!

MORE RESOURCES

See videos & more resources at *abundantlifestudy.com*.

Video 1	Introduction
Video 2	Part I Overview
Video 3	Week 1
Video 4	Salvation Evaluation
Video 5	Week 2
Video 6	Week 3
Video 7	Week 4
Video 8	Part II Overview
Video 9	Week 5
Video 10	Week 6
Video 11	Heart Examination
Video 12	Part III Overview
Videos 13-15	Weeks 7-10
Video 16	Conclusion

See videos & more
under resources at
abundantlifestudy.com

THE ABUNDANT LIFE PATHWAY

The figure on the next page summarizes The Abundant Life pathway. It all starts with abundant revelation from the Word of God. This revelation of the grace of God is so amazing and incredible that the believer then has an abundant response to God which is initiated through surrender. The abundant response of the believer to God's revelation results in God responding back. This sets up a feedback loop creating an abundant relationship, which defines the abundant state of spiritual health. The abundant results are the natural outflow and result of abundant health. All of these feed back into each other, creating a continuing cycle of increasing spiritual growth, health, and results.

The more we learn about our Heavenly Father and Lord Jesus Christ, the more we respond and grow in Him, which opens up more room for the cycle to continue. We fall deeper and deeper in love and are increasingly amazed at the Person and work of God in our lives. The more we grow and know, the more we surrender and serve from gratitude, awe, and wonder.

PART I
ABUNDANT REVELATION

PART II
ABUNDANT RESPONSE

ABUNDANT HEALTH

PART III
ABUNDANT RESULTS

See videos & more
under resources at
abundantlifestudy.com

OUTLINE

Part I. Abundant Revelation
Abundant Grace:

WEEK 1
- Abundant Need
- Abundant Provision
- **Salvation Evaluation**

WEEK 2
- Abundant Change
- Abundant Newness
- Abundant Worth

WEEK 3
- Abundant Wealth
- Abundant Power
- Abundant Freedom

WEEK 4
- Abundant Security
- Abundant Hope
- Abundant Plans

Part II. Abundant Response (God & Man)
Abundant Relationship:

WEEK 5
- Abundant Surrender
- Abundant Praise
- Abundant Words

WEEK 6
- Abundant God
- Abundant Repentance
- Abundant Love for God
- Abundant Health
- **Heart Examination**

Part III. Abundant Results
Abundant Transformation:

WEEK 7
- Abundant Growth
- Abundant Godliness

WEEK 8
- Abundant Struggle
- Abundant Suffering
- Abundant Victory

Abundant Fruit:

WEEK 9
- Abundant Love for Others
- Abundant Giving

WEEK 10
- Abundant Service
- Abundant Harvest

PART I
ABUNDANT REVELATION
Abundant Grace

WEEK 1

LESSON 1 • **ABUNDANT NEED:** THE NEED FOR GRACE

LESSON 2 • **ABUNDANT PROVISION:** THE RESCUE OF GRACE

→ **SALVATION EVALUATION** ←

WEEK 2

LESSON 3 • **ABUNDANT CHANGE:** THE RESULTS OF GRACE

LESSON 4 • **ABUNDANT NEWNESS:** THE TRANSFORMATION OF GRACE

LESSON 5 • **ABUNDANT WORTH:** THE WORTHINESS OF GRACE

WEEK 3

LESSON 6 • **ABUNDANT WEALTH:** THE RICHES OF GRACE

LESSON 7 • **ABUNDANT POWER:** THE EMPOWERMENT OF GRACE

LESSON 8 • **ABUNDANT FREEDOM:** THE LIBERTY OF GRACE

WEEK 4

LESSON 9 • **ABUNDANT SECURITY:** THE SAFETY OF GRACE

LESSON 10 • **ABUNDANT HOPE:** THE CERTAINTY OF GRACE

LESSON 11 • **ABUNDANT PLANS:** THE DETAILS OF GRACE

See videos & more
under resources at
abundantlifestudy.com

ABUNDANT NEED
The Need for Grace

$\twoheadleftarrow\twoheadleftarrow$

You were dead in your transgressions and sins.
Ephesians 2:1 NIV

The starting point to begin experiencing the abundant life is a realization of the depravity of the human condition, our condition before salvation. The more we understand how lost and dead in sin we were before salvation, the more grateful we will be for God's incredible provision of His Son.

If we have a debt that we cannot pay, $100 for example, and someone voluntarily pays it off, we would certainly be grateful. Now if that debt were $1,000,000, we would be flabbergasted and amazed at that person's kindness. However, let us suppose that debt is for something other than money and, in fact, was for our very life and even our soul. First, we would likely think that no one would or could pay that for us, but what if he could and did? What if the person paid for our life with his own? How awesome would that be? Well, as a Christian, that is exactly what Jesus did for us. He gave His life for ours and paid the penalty for our sins. This allowed us to be reconciled with God and become saved. Christians should be abundantly grateful!

In this lesson we will study the abundant need for salvation because of abundant sin. Every Christian should regularly reflect on their fallen state before salvation. This will accomplish three important things:

1. Hinder religious pride and self-righteousness as we begin to have a successful Christian life. It should keep us humble.

See videos & more under resources at abundantlifestudy.com

17

2. Create within us a heart for the lost who do not understand what grave danger they are living in each day. We need to remember that we used to be lost and in this same condition. This reflection will give us more compassion and empathy.

3. Create a grateful heart of love and devotion for God who paid our debt. The monumental extent and cost of that payment will be explored in the next lesson.

VERSES TO READ, STUDY, AND MEDITATE ON:

1. **You were born in a state of sin.** *Psalm 51:5; Romans 3:23, 5:12-21; Ephesians 2:1-3*

2. **You were spiritually dead** *(separated from God). Romans 6:23; Ephesians 2:1-3; Colossians 2:13; Isaiah 59:2*

3. **You were spiritually blind.** *2 Corinthians 4:3-4; Ephesians 4:17-19; 1 John 2:11*

4. **You were spiritually deaf.** *Matthew 13:13-15; 1 John 4:6*

5. **You were lost and perishing** *(being destroyed). Luke 19:10; 1 Corinthians 1:18 (see also: 2 Corinthians 2:15-16, 4:3. This format will be used throughout the study to designate additional verses that are optional to study.)*

6. **You were held captive by Satan to do his will.** *2 Timothy 2:24-26*

7. **You were not a good person.** *Romans 1:18-2:16, 3:9-20, 7:18 (Isaiah 53:6; Ecclesiastes 7:20)*

8. **Your good works were like filthy rags.** This means that even our very best good works were stained with sin and unable to earn us favor with God. *Isaiah 64:6*

9. **Your heart was desperately wicked.** *Jeremiah 17:9; Mark 7:20-21; Galatians 5:19-21*

10. **You were a slave to sin.** *John 8:34-36; Romans 6:6, 20*

11. **You had no hope.** *Ephesians 2:11-12*

12. **You were already condemned to hell and eternal death.** *John 3:18; Revelation 20:11-15; Ezekiel 18:4*

SUMMARY

Prior to salvation, you were spiritually dead, a condemned sinner, and a slave with an eternal debt on eternal death row.

QUESTIONS TO PONDER:

1. It is obvious that the human creation is more fallen than we can comprehend. Use the following analogy to discuss the fall of man:

   If a boulder falls from a high cliff and gets broken into many pieces on the ground, then what is necessary for complete restoration to its starting position in its original form? What is necessary for the task of reconstruction and restoration? Isn't this process of reconstruction and restoration much more complicated than the original fall? Relate this to the fall of man from sin and what must happen to restore us. Ponder the fact that we are so used to seeing the broken pieces that we often forget that we are fallen and broken.

2. If we were born spiritually dead, deaf, and blind from sin, then what needs to happen to us at salvation? Will salvation only involve the forgiveness of sins or much more?

See videos & more
under resources at
abundantlifestudy.com

3. Sin is complicated. Ponder and discuss how many ways there are to do something in a sinful manner versus the right way. Consider how you can do wrong in many different ways by not doing something (i.e., failing to act).

4. Discuss how a person can have a secretly selfish motive behind an outwardly good deed. Can a person be nice but with an impure motive? Can a person act and appear religious but have a selfish motive? Can you relate this to Cain from Genesis chapter 4? Why did Cain even bother to bring an offering? Read and investigate.

5. Since everyone (even mature Christians) continues to sin and makes mistakes on a daily basis, what is the ongoing need for the grace and mercy of God in our lives? Many Christians claim that they are more and more aware of their sins and their many levels as they mature in the Christian life. Would this increase the awareness of our need for grace and mercy and, as a result, make us more grateful for what Christ has done?

See videos & more
under resources at
abundantlifestudy.com

ABUNDANT PROVISION
The Rescue of Grace

❮❮❮❮

*But God, who is rich in mercy, because of His
great love with which He loved us, even when we
were dead in trespasses, made us alive together
with Christ (by grace you have been saved).*
Ephesians 2:4-5 NKJV

In the last lesson we examined the debt of mankind because of sin. Now
we are going to learn the price paid for that debt. A careful examination of
what God had to do to redeem man will also give us more insight into the
depravity of man due to sin. The price paid will reveal the magnitude of the debt
from another perspective. A proper understanding of both sides of salvation will
provide the fuel, spark, and fire for the abundant life.

VERSES TO READ, STUDY, AND MEDITATE ON:

1. **Jesus Christ, the eternal Son of God, became the God-man (God in
   the flesh) from Heaven to be our substitute because of God's mercy,
   love, and grace.** Jesus is fully man and fully God. He is perfectly
   sinless humanity and deity united in one person forever! Only as a
   man could He physically die, and only as God would His death have
   infinite value that was sufficient to provide redemption for the sins
   of the whole world. *John 1:1-18, 3:13-17, 14:9-11; Philippians 2:5-11;
   1 Timothy 3:16; Hebrews 2:10-18*

See videos & more
under resources at
abundantlifestudy.com

23

2. **Jesus lived a sinless life and kept God's law perfectly.** As we shall see, it is His sinless life and perfect obedience to God's law that allowed His sacrifice to become the basis for our righteousness. God is able to declare us righteous because of what Jesus accomplished—if we believe Jesus is God and have accepted His free gift of salvation. *Romans 5:19; 2 Corinthians 5:21; Hebrews 4:15; 1 Peter 1:19, 2:22-23 (John 8:46; Hebrews 7:26, 9:14; 1 John 3:5)*

3. **Jesus was crucified as the perfect Lamb of God for the sins of the world according to the Old Testament Scriptures.** *Isaiah chapter 53; John 1:29; Acts 2:22-36; 1 Corinthians 15:3-4; 1 Peter 1:18-19; 1 John 2:2*

4. **Jesus died in our place, taking the punishment and penalty for our sins on Himself.** The cross is personal for every one of us in that God died for everyone. Jesus did not die on behalf of everyone. He died in place of each individual. He did it for you personally. *Isaiah 53:6, 12; Romans 5:6-8; 2 Corinthians 5:21; Galatians 3:13; 1 Timothy 2:5-6; 1 Peter 2:24 (Titus 2:13; 1 Peter 3:18)*

5. **The sacrifice of Jesus Christ as the God-man on the cross was a sacrifice of atonement that satisfied and turned away the wrath of God against sin (propitiation).** Jesus satisfied the holy wrath of God's righteousness against sin by bearing the penalty Himself. This only practically applies for those who accept God's salvation. God's wrath is still in place for those who do not. *Romans 3:25; 1 John 2:2, 4:10 (Hebrews 2:17)*

6. **Jesus suffered the wrath of God and was forsaken by the Father on the cross to purchase our salvation.** The night before He suffered and died for us, He knew the cost and He was in agony to the point of sweat that was like blood. Jesus never sinned but took the punishment for our sins as if He had. He was an innocent, willing substitute. *Matthew 27:46; Luke 22:41-44 (Mark 15:34; 2 Corinthians 5:21)*

7. **Jesus died, was buried, and rose again the third day proving He was victorious and that He is God.** *John chapter 20; 1 Corinthians 15:3-8; Acts 10:40*

QUESTIONS TO PONDER:

1. Since Jesus took the place of all humanity on the cross, the crucifixion becomes a mirror to the magnitude of our depravity and consequences of sin. Read *Isaiah 52:14; Matthew 27:27-31, 45-51; Luke 22:63-64; and John 19:1-2*. What does this teach us about sin and what God had to go through to provide a way for us to be saved?

2. Read *Luke 22:41-44*. What could make Jesus, the God-man, while in agony, sweat blood the night before He was facing the crucifixion? What does this tell us about the price He had to pay for sin? What does this tell us about the depth of our depravity? Read *Matthew 27:45-26*. The crucifixion was a horrible event for Jesus to endure for us, but what was the far greater agony that He endured on the cross?

3. How great is God's love and mercy, based upon the verses we have read? Read *Ephesians 3:14-19*.

See videos & more under resources at abundantlifestudy.com

26

SALVATION EVALUATION

SALVATION
EVALUATION

—‹‹‹‹

*Examine yourselves to see whether you are in the
faith. Test yourselves. Do you not realize
that Christ Jesus is in you—unless,
of course, you fail the test?*
2 Corinthians 13:5 NIV

This Bible study was designed for genuine born again Christians. You
cannot even begin to experience the abundant life unless you have been
genuinely saved by Jesus Christ. Born again, regenerated, and saved
are all synonyms for salvation. At this point, we have reviewed God's plan of
salvation and the need for it. It is important for us to make sure we are not
deceived about our salvation. Why? Because Jesus delivered a grave warning
about this very issue. He warned that many people who are convinced they are
Christians are not. They even call Him Lord, a title of authority over their lives,
but they have not been saved.

> *"Not everyone who says to Me, 'Lord, Lord,' shall enter the kingdom of
> heaven, but he who does the will of My Father in heaven. Many will say to
> Me in that day, 'Lord, Lord, have we not prophesied in Your name, cast out
> demons in Your name, and done many wonders in Your name?' And then I
> will declare to them, 'I never knew you; depart from Me, you who practice
> lawlessness!'"* Matthew 7:21-23 NKJV

Read the following verses carefully and ask God to reveal to you where you
stand with Him. Notice that the signs of a genuine Christian, according to Jesus'
words above, are doing the will of the Father and having a personal, interactive
relationship with Him. Do you pass His test?

> *Jesus answered and said to him, "Most assuredly, I say to you, unless one is
> born again, he cannot see the kingdom of God." John 3:3 NKJV*

See videos & more
under resources at
abundantlifestudy.com

For all have sinned and fall short of the glory of God. For the wages of sin is death, but the gift of God is eternal life in Christ Jesus our Lord. Romans 3:23, 6:23 NKJV

For God so loved the world that He gave His only begotten Son, that whoever believes in Him should not perish but have everlasting life. John 3:16 NKJV

For what I received I passed on to you as of first importance: that Christ died for our sins according to the Scriptures, that he was buried, that he was raised on the third day according to the Scriptures, and that he appeared to Peter, and then to the Twelve. After that, he appeared to more than five hundred of the brothers at the same time, most of whom are still living, though some have fallen asleep. Then he appeared to James, then to all the apostles, and last of all he appeared to me also, as to one abnormally born. 1 Corinthians 15:3-8 NIV

"The word is near you; it is in your mouth and in your heart," that is, the word of faith we are proclaiming: That if you confess with your mouth, "Jesus is Lord," and believe in your heart that God raised him from the dead, you will be saved. For it is with your heart that you believe and are justified, and it is with your mouth that you confess and are saved. As the Scripture says, "Anyone who trusts in him will never be put to shame." For there is no difference between Jew and Gentile—the same Lord is Lord of all and richly blesses all who call on him, for, "Everyone who calls on the name of the Lord will be saved." Romans 10:8-13 NIV

For it is by grace you have been saved, through faith—and this not from yourselves, it is the gift of God—not by works, so that no one can boast. Ephesians 2:8-9 NIV

You can pray to God right now and receive Jesus as your Savior, but it is critical that you truly believe and understand how to be saved. There is a lot of "easy believism" Christianity today, wherein people come to Jesus for the wrong reasons and think they are saved when they are not.

Salvation is a free gift from God. You cannot earn it by good behavior or receive it from any religious institution or classes. It is a transaction between you and

God that comes from the heart. The Bible is clear that you must believe in Jesus Christ to be saved, but what does that mean? What does "believe" mean when used in the Bible? The word "believe" in the Bible goes far beyond intellectual assent. A person can intellectually believe that Jesus is the Savior and that He died for their sins but not be a Christian. A person can "believe in God" and go right to hell.

> *You believe that there is one God. You do well. Even the demons believe— and tremble! James 2:19 NKJV*

True Biblical belief involves the heart and not just the mind. It describes a continual faith and trust that is put into action. It is the difference between looking at a medicine and intellectually understanding that it is a real medicine that works, and actually swallowing the pill and trusting in it to cure you. You can hold the real cure for a disease in your hand and intellectually understand that it can cure you, but you must take it inside your body for it to work and produce changes. Biblical believing is an ongoing state of faith and trust in Jesus as Savior from the heart. It results in action. Faith and believing in the Bible are different forms of the same Greek word. Faith is the noun, and believing is the verb.

Believing in Jesus also means that you believe the right things about Him and why He came. He is God incarnate (the God-man), who came to die for the sins of the world because we all have sinned and are dead in our sins (separated from God) without Jesus Christ. Jesus Christ died in our place and was raised the third day conquering death thus proving He is God. A man cannot be saved if he does not believe Jesus is God. Believing in Jesus means we understand that we are lost sinners with no other way of salvation. We understand that we have sinned against God and repent. Repentance is essential to salvation and is part of "believing" in Jesus.

> *[Jesus said] "I tell you, no; but unless you repent you will all likewise perish." Luke 13:3 NKJV*

> *Repent therefore and be converted, that your sins may be blotted out, so that times of refreshing may come from the presence of the Lord. Acts 3:19 NKJV*

See videos & more under resources at abundantlifestudy.com

Truly, these times of ignorance God overlooked, but now commands all men everywhere to repent. Acts 17:30 NKJV

Repentance is the second critical aspect of salvation. Like believing, repentance is a state of the heart, not just the mind. It is absolutely essential for salvation. This is a critical aspect of salvation that is not only widely misunderstood but also under-preached in many churches today. What does it mean to truly repent?

- Admit you are a sinner who has sinned against God, in need of forgiveness and change. This is an acknowledgement to God of your sinfulness with a desire to change.

- Turn away from your sins and turn towards God for change. It is conviction in the heart that causes a turn to Jesus Christ. It is an act of the will and a change of heart that go in a reverse direction that will result in actions and a changed life.

- Repentance is an integral part of believing and having faith in Jesus. Believing and faith result in changing one's mind and heart about Jesus and seeing the need for Jesus because of who He is and what He has done. This absolutely involves the recognition of the need and willingness for change. In this sense, repentance is an aspect of "believing."

STUDY THIS VERSE CAREFULLY.

Two different translations are given.

For the kind of sorrow God wants us to experience leads us away from sin and results in salvation. There's no regret for that kind of sorrow. But worldly sorrow, which lacks repentance, results in spiritual death. 2 Corinthians 7:10 NLT

For godly sorrow produces repentance leading to salvation, not to be regretted; but the sorrow of the world produces death. 2 Corinthians 7:10 NKJV

How is repentance different from being sorry for sin or being remorseful? Repentance is God-centered, not self-centered. A repentant heart sees sin in light of a holy God and desires to change. It understands that forgiveness is needed from God. A sorrowful or remorseful heart is upset from the consequences of its actions and the negative impacts it has caused for self and others. Remorse feels bad but does not result in change, and a person will likely repeat sinning, especially if consequences can be avoided.

Repentance is a turning away from sin and towards God for both forgiveness and change. A person can intellectually acknowledge their sin before God and not repent. They can confess they have sinned without any repentance in their heart, but God knows their true heart.

Salvation is a specific moment in time when you personally trust and believe in Jesus Christ to save you. You must have a Biblical belief in Jesus and salvation. Your heart is repentant and desires to change and turn away from a selfish lifestyle of sin and towards God and a relationship with Him. This is a personal confession of sin, a desire to change, an acknowledgement that Jesus is your Savior, and that you accept His free gift. This is not a rehearsed or taught event in a person's life from a religious class. It is a commitment to Him as best you understand at that point in time.

What is important are not the exact words that a person says but what is in his or her heart. A person is not saved by reciting a magical prayer or set of words. Simply repeating a "sinner's prayer" does not save anyone. God does the saving and is looking at the heart. A person can technically "call on the Lord" for salvation without uttering an audible word. The heart does the calling, and the heart is what God is concerned about.

Even though the actual transaction of salvation is a specific moment in time, many people may not be able to pinpoint this event. Some people were saved as a child, while others are not sure exactly when they truly trusted in Christ to save them. This is okay, but we must be careful to ensure that people are not trusting in their Christian religion, rituals, or church attendance as evidence of their salvation. On the other hand, some people are saved but are not certain of their salvation because they are not living the abundant life.

See videos & more under resources at abundantlifestudy.com

At this point you need to make sure you really believe in Jesus Christ as your Savior. You need to evaluate what you really believe and whether or not you are saved. There are certain things you must believe that can be used as a test to evaluate yourself:

- Do you believe that there is only one God and that Jesus is fully God and equal to the Father?

- Do you believe that Jesus is the Savior and that He died on the cross for your sins and then was resurrected to life again the third day?

- Do you understand that you have sinned, are a sinner, and because of this you cannot ever in your own strength or behavior be united with God? No one, not one single person, will ever be "good enough" to get to Heaven, because a person would have to live a perfectly sinless life and the only person to do that or will ever do that is Jesus.

- Do you believe that Jesus is the only way to be saved? Do you believe that there is nothing you can do to be accepted by God except receiving Jesus as Savior? You cannot be good enough or earn your way into Heaven by good deeds or behavior. Christian religion, rituals, and things such as baptism and confirmation do not save you. A person is not saved by going to church and being a "good" person. Are you trusting in Jesus and His work on the cross to save you, or are you trusting in yourself and your Christian religious behavior and institution to save you?

- Do you have a daily personal relationship with God through Jesus Christ? Is He guiding your life and slowly changing you? Are you in relationship with Him through prayer, worship, and reading His Word? Are you doing His personal will for your life? Jesus defines eternal life as knowing God and being known by God in a relationship. This results in doing the will of the Father.

"Not everyone who says to Me, 'Lord, Lord,' shall enter the kingdom of heaven, but he who does the will of My Father in heaven. Many will say to Me in that day, 'Lord, Lord, have we not prophesied in Your name, cast out demons in Your name, and done many wonders in Your name?' And then I will declare to them, 'I never knew you; depart from Me, you who practice lawlessness!' " Matthew 7:21-23 NKJV

And this is eternal life, that they may know You, the only true God, and Jesus Christ whom You have sent. John 17:3 NKJV

If you do believe but are uncertain of your salvation, then cry out to Jesus for salvation. Repent and turn to Him for eternal life. He gave His life to save yours and give you eternal life that starts now. If you have trusted in Christian religion, rituals, sacraments, or a religious upbringing, then repent and turn to God now to start your relationship with Him. He loves you and wants to save you right now. You will know if something is wrong. The Holy Spirit will be working on your heart to convict you of sin and draw you to Jesus Christ. Do not turn the page until you receive Jesus as your personal Savior right now. Then begin the abundant life and be certain forever!

Remember that God desperately wants to save you. He gave his Son so that your sins could be forgiven, so if you come to Him, He will not turn you down. Do not get tripped up on technicalities. If you truly seek God and cry out for salvation, you will be saved. And your level of belief is not measured against others. God simply wants you to believe in Him as much as you know how at the moment you give yourself to Him. Surrender to God and He will take care of the rest. As you grow in the Lord, your faith and belief will increase. Once you have done this, do not doubt God. He has promised to save you, and once you are saved, you will be securely held in the hand of God forever!

See videos & more
under resources at
abundantlifestudy.com

REFLECTIONS
Week 1

Spend some time in prayer reflecting on this week's lessons. Ask God to speak to your heart and reveal to you what's important. Then spend some time answering the questions below. Write down your responses to discuss them in your small groups or as a journal entry to remember what you have learned.

INSIGHTS:

What are some of the key insights you have learned from this week's lessons? What has stood out to you? What has spoken to your heart?

Lesson 1 • Abundant Need

Lesson 2 • Abundant Provision

Salvation Evaluation

APPLICATIONS:

How should you respond to what you have learned in this week's lessons?
What do you need to do differently? What changes do you feel the Lord
leading you to make? What specific steps can you take?

See videos & more
under resources at
abundantlifestudy.com

ABUNDANT CHANGE
The Results of Grace

↞↞↞↞

*In Him we have redemption through His blood, the forgiveness
of sins, according to the riches of His grace which He made to
abound toward us in all wisdom and prudence.*
Ephesians 1:7-8 NKJV

This lesson will begin to highlight some of the incredible changes that take place at the moment of salvation. We will continue to explore these for several more lessons since there are so many of them! It is my experience that many Christians have no idea of the incredible and radical changes and blessings that occur from accepting Jesus Christ as Savior. A lot of people think He only came to provide forgiveness of sins and a ticket to Heaven ("get out of hell free" card), but He accomplished so much more. Christianity is not something you believe but someone you become. God radically changes the nature of your existence when you are saved. The more we understand the incredible grace and provision of God, the more motivated we will be to serve Him and surrender our lives to Him from gratitude, awe, wonder, and love.

VERSES TO READ, STUDY, AND MEDITATE ON:

1. **God wiped clean the record of your sin, and He even destroyed the record book.** Your sin is not only forgiven but forgotten. *Psalm 103:12; Isaiah 43:25; Micah 7:19; Ephesians 1:4-8; Colossians 1:21-22, 2:13-15*

See videos & more
under resources at
abundantlifestudy.com

2. **God has declared you righteous.** God credits the righteousness of Jesus Christ to your account. God gives you a sinless, perfect standing in His sight even though, practically, you will continue to sin and make mistakes. This is known as being justified or justification. You stand in the grace of God. *Isaiah 61:10; Romans 3:21-26, 5:1-2; 2 Corinthians 5:21; Philippians 3:8-9 (1 Corinthians 1:30; Titus 3:4-7)*

3. **You are in Christ. God has placed you "in Christ."** This means when He looks upon you He sees the perfect righteousness of His Son, the Lord Jesus Christ. This is positional and not practical, since we all continue to sin and make mistakes. *Romans 8:1; 1 Corinthians 1:30; 2 Corinthians 5:17; Ephesians 1:3-14, 2:6*

4. **Christ is in you.** God now dwells within your existence by His Holy Spirit in your heart. *John 14:17-20, 17:20-26; Romans 8:9-11; 1 Corinthians 3:16; Galatians 2:20-21; Colossians 1:27 (2 Timothy 1:14; 1 John 4:4, 13)*

5. **Jesus Christ has redeemed you by His blood.** The Greek word for redemption means to buy out of the slave market. Jesus bought you out of the slave market of sin by purchasing you with His blood. Jesus died so that He could purchase your freedom. Your debt is fully paid. *Romans 3:21-24; 1 Corinthians 6:19-20; Galatians 3:13; Ephesians 1:7; Colossians 1:14 (Acts 20:28; Galatians 4:5; Hebrews 9:11-15; 1 Peter 1:18-19; Revelation 5:9-10)*

6. **God has given you eternal life that starts now.** You have been made spiritually alive by the Holy Spirit living within you. You were spiritually dead, but now you are spiritually alive forever. You were separated from God but are now united with Him forever. *John 5:24-25, 10:28; Romans 6:23; Ephesians 2:1-3; Colossians 2:13-14; 1 John 5:11-13 (1 Corinthians 15:21-22; 1 John 2:25)*

QUESTIONS TO PONDER:

1. Read *Psalm 103:12*. Why did God choose to say east and west instead of north and south? Discuss the difference between your sins being just forgiven and both forgiven and forgotten. How big of a difference is this? Why did God do it this way?

2. God has forgiven and forgotten your sins and given you the righteousness of Christ (God). If you have the righteousness of God and are in Christ, what can be added to this?

    Can you become more saved than having the righteousness of God in your account?

    Can you become more righteous in God's eyes than what He has already given you?

    Can you earn more favor than He has already given you? Is there an elite club of God for the spiritually serious who receive special favor from Him?

    If you have a good day and do good deeds, have you added to your righteousness with God?

    If you have a bad day, have you lost righteousness?

See videos & more
under resources at
abundantlifestudy.com

3. Ponder and discuss how God living within you by the Holy Spirit, who is God, enables you to have an intimate personal relationship with Him. Discuss the difference between God living within your existence and if He were only in Heaven and interacted with you from there.

4. Think deeply and discuss redemption. Why would someone go to a slave market to buy someone out of slavery? Jesus saw you there and wanted to set you free. God counted the cost and sent Jesus Christ to die as the God-man to buy your freedom. This is an incomprehensible price. What should our response be once we have been purchased and set free? What does "counted the cost" mean for God?

See videos & more
under resources at
abundantlifestudy.com

ABUNDANT NEWNESS
The Transformation of Grace

—‹‹‹‹‹

*Therefore, if anyone is in Christ, he is a new
creation; old things have passed away;
behold, all things have become new.*
2 Corinthians 5:17 NKJV

This lesson will continue to explore the amazing and radical changes that occur as a result of being saved by Jesus Christ. In Lesson 3 we learned that God actually now lives inside of us, but there are also many other changes to our existence and relationship with God. God has made many things new in His plan of salvation for mankind. As you read, study, and meditate on these concepts and Scriptures, ask God to reveal to you what an amazing process salvation really is.

VERSES TO READ, STUDY, AND MEDITATE ON:

1. **The Old Man is Dead.** The old you died with Jesus Christ when you accepted Him as your Savior. In a way that we cannot comprehend but Scripture makes clear, the old man dies and remains dead. The old person is somehow united in the death of Jesus. It is as if you were actually crucified with Jesus and died with Him. *Galatians 2:20; Romans 6:5-8; Colossians 3:3*

See videos & more
under resources at
abundantlifestudy.com

2. **The New Man is Created.** When a person receives Jesus Christ, God creates an entirely new person. The old man is crucified with Christ and dies, but then God raises up a new person to live a new life. This new man has a new nature. He is inclined to know God and live in fellowship and obedience to Him, versus the old man whose natural inclination was rebellion. *Romans 6:4-5; Colossians 3:9-10; Ephesians 4:20-24*

3. **The New Birth.** The new man God created when you were saved is actually a spiritual baby. You were born again as a new creation in Christ (spiritual baby). *John 1:12-13, 3:3; Titus 3:4-5; 1 Peter 1:3, 2:2; 1 John 3:9*

4. **The New Creation.** The new birth creates a new man who is a new creation with a new heart and mind. *2 Corinthians 5:17; Galatians 6:15*

5. **The New Heart.** Your spirit/soul, the source of the real person, is the same as your heart/mind. When a person is saved by Jesus Christ he or she receives a "new heart." A newly created person will have a new heart. A new heart enables us to have the capacity to love God and others. *Ezekiel 36:26-27; Romans 5:5*

6. **The New Mind.** Not only do we get a new heart but also a new mind. The indwelling of the Holy Spirit, who is God, within a person's existence not only connects our mind with God's, but also gives us the ability to discern, understand, and learn spiritual things from the Bible and learn the will of God. With a new mind we can know God. *1 Corinthians 2:10-16; John 14:26; 1 John 2:20, 27; 1 Peter 4:1-6*

7. **The New Relationship.** Jesus Christ has reconciled you to God. Your relationship with God has been restored to one of peace and Fatherly love. You are fully and unconditionally accepted by God. *Romans 5:10-11; 2 Corinthians 5:18-21; Colossians 1:20-22; Ephesians 1:6, 2:14-18*

8. **The New Family.** God has adopted you as a child of God into the family and kingdom of God. *John 1:12-13; Romans 8:14-17; Galatians 3:26, 4:5; Ephesians 1:5; Colossians 1:13*

9. **The New Citizenship.** God has made you a citizen of Heaven. You are no longer of this world. You live in this world but you are no longer of it. You are now passing through on your way to Heaven. *Philippians 3:20; Hebrews 11:13-16; Ephesians 2:19; John 15:19, 17:14-16*

QUESTIONS TO PONDER:

1. Given all of the results of salvation, is it possible for a person to be saved and born again and yet show no signs of change in their life over a period of time? Ponder this question and discuss.

2. When you are born again you become a spiritual baby. What does a baby need to do to grow and mature? What if a baby only eats once a week? Does a baby know he is a baby? Ponder this spiritual analogy and the need for spiritual growth and maturation that will be covered later in Part II.

3. Reread the Scriptures from #9 above. Discuss how being a citizen of Heaven and not of this world should change your paradigm of life and priorities here on earth. If you were visiting a foreign country for a short period of time, for example, how would you live there differently than if you thought that it was your final destination/residence?

4. Read *Romans 5:10-11*. What is the difference between being an enemy of God and being His child? Discuss this monumental shift in relationship. Make a table and contrast the two.

See videos & more
under resources at
abundantlifestudy.com

ABUNDANT WORTH
The Worthiness of Grace

—≪≪≪≪

You are the light of the world.
Matthew 5:14 NIV

In the last lesson we learned that we are a completely new person and creation in Christ after being born again at the moment of salvation. This new person is "in Christ." As sinners who were enemies of God and have now become children of God, we are still not worthy of any of God's love and blessings. That is why it is all God's grace! God has gone much further, however, and made us important and valuable people in Christ. This lesson reviews who we are in Christ, or our personage in Christ. God has declared that we are very valuable to Him, and He has revealed that as Christians we have important roles and responsibilities. This should be very comforting, exciting, humbling, and motivating because we do not deserve any of it. There is zero room for a Christian to feel unworthy any longer. Yes, we should remember that we are not worthy of the grace given to us and be very humble before God, but we should also be very confident, excited, and blessed because God has given us abundant worthiness by His grace.

VERSES TO READ, STUDY, AND MEDITATE ON:

1. **You are God's workmanship.** The Greek word for workmanship is poema, from which we get our word poem. This means you are God's special masterpiece and work of beauty that He has custom designed and created for His glory. He has a unique plan for you and thinks about you all the time. *Ephesians 2:10; Psalm 139:13-18; Isaiah 64:8; Luke 12:7 (2 Timothy 1:9; Psalm 138:8)*

See videos & more under resources at abundantlifestudy.com

49

2. **You are God's ambassador.** God has made you ambassador of His plan of salvation in Jesus Christ (the Gospel), and entrusted you with the ministry of reconciliation. The Lord wants to use you to plead with others to be saved and become children of God. You are the representative of Jesus Christ and should share what He did to save you from your sins and eternal death. *2 Corinthians 5:18-21; Ephesians 6:19-20*

3. **You are God's child.** We have already learned that we have been adopted into the family of God as His children, but it is worth reviewing again! *1 John 3:1-3 (John 1:12-13; Romans 8:14-17)*

4. **You are God's temple.** This is an incredible reference to the temple of the Old Testament where God's glory literally dwelt. God has revealed to us that now we are that temple! He lives inside each and every one of us. A temple is a place that is dedicated to God, and it is to be kept holy or set apart for the use of God. This is an amazing blessing and honor. *1 Corinthians 6:19-20 (John 2:19-21; 1 Corinthians 3:16-17; 2 Corinthians 6:16)*

5. **You are God's priest.** There is no more need for an intermediary between man and God because of what Jesus has done. You can go directly to God. This term may be a stumbling block for some people because they immediately think of the priests of formal Christian religion. The Word of God, however, clearly calls every Christian a priest. Priests in the Old Testament served an important purpose of representing God to the people. They would help people come to God and show them what to do. For us, this means we are to be priests of our homes and to the lost who do not have a saving relationship with Jesus Christ. If another believer is struggling in his or her relationship with the Lord, we should help that person get back on the right path. Priests should also know the Word of God (Bible) very well to give proper instructions. Ponder the role of priests in the Old Testament books Leviticus and Numbers. *1 Peter 2:5-10; Revelation 1:5-6, 5:10*

6. **You are God's saint.** This is another term that, by its name, may cause confusion. Christian religion has made saints of certain people after they have died to commemorate their service. The Bible, however, calls every Christian a saint while they are alive! It is used 61 times in the

New Testament. It means we are set apart to the service of God and devoted to Him. You are a saint! (Some newer translations substitute "holy people" for the word saints.) *1 Corinthians 1:1-4; Philippians 1:1 (Romans 1:7; Ephesians 1:1)*

7. **You are the salt of the earth.** Salt provides flavor and healing and creates thirst. It also preserves. *Matthew 5:13 (Colossians 4:6)*

8. **You are a light in the world.** Light shines in the darkness so that people can see. *Matthew 5:14-16; Ephesians 5:8-14 (John 12:35-36)*

9. **You are being conformed to the image of Christ.** One of the goals and purposes of the Christian life is a slow process in which we are transformed into the likeness of Jesus Christ. This means that over time you are to become more like Jesus in your life. This is called sanctification and will be discussed in a future lesson. For now, you simply need to understand that it is an amazing plan of God's. *Romans 8:29-30; 2 Corinthians 3:18*

10. **You are God's chosen.** Every person who has been saved has been chosen by God. The Bible is clear that you were chosen before the foundation of the world. This is an incomprehensible fact. The theology of these verses is highly controversial and will not be explored in this study. All of the verses you will read were written to believers, not the unsaved. Some facts that God gives us should be rejoiced over and left as incomprehensible facts that we cannot figure out. They were written to encourage believers in the Lord. Be encouraged! *John 15:16; Romans 8:29-30; Ephesians 1:3-6 (2 Thessalonians 2:13-14)*

11. **You are abundantly loved by God.** He died for you! He created you and cares for you more than you can ever comprehend. Look to the cross and see His love. It is perfect and unconditional. *Jeremiah 31:3; John 3:16, 15:13; 17:23; Romans 5:6-8; Ephesians 3:17-19; 1 John 3:1, 4:7-11*

12. **You are more than a conqueror in Christ.** This means you are a super conqueror who has surpassing victory! *Romans 8:37-39; 2 Corinthians 2:14; 1 John 5:4*

See videos & more under resources at abundantlifestudy.com

13. You are a member of the body of Christ. The moment a person is saved that person is placed into union with Jesus Christ and is joined to the body of Christ. *1 Corinthians 12:12-14, 27; Ephesians 1:22-23, 5:30*

14. You are the bride of Christ. The church is the spiritual bride of Christ. We are engaged to Jesus! *Ephesians 5:25-33; Revelation 19:7-9, 21:9 (John 3:29)*

QUESTIONS TO PONDER:

1. In *1 Corinthians 1:1-4*, Paul calls those in the church at Corinth saints. This church was immature, in sin, and not living a Godly lifestyle. This church had many problems including sexual immorality. How can Paul call them saints? Relate this to what you have learned about being in Christ and declared righteous.

2. What is an ambassador? What is their role and what authority do they have? Discuss how Christians are ambassadors for Christ and His plan for salvation.

3. Reread *Matthew 5:13*. What does salt do? How does salt accomplish its purposes? How important was salt 2000 years ago? What would the people hearing this from Jesus think? Was Jesus telling them they are important? Does salt need to have contact or can it function in the shaker? Relate this analogy to Jesus calling us the salt of the earth. As salt, what are we supposed to do? What did Jesus mean by His warning in this verse?

4. Discuss and ponder the blessings and responsibilities of being the temple of God. Discuss how sacrifice, cleansing, worship, praise, and prayer should be a part of your individual Christian life. If you are a personal temple in which God dwells, how does this fact make Christianity a personal relationship? What would the Jews living in the Old Testament times, where only one person (the high priest) could go into the presence of God one time per year (the day of atonement), think of this? How excited do you think they would be that so many barriers to intimacy with the living God have been removed?

See videos & more
under resources at
abundantlifestudy.com

REFLECTIONS
Week 2

Spend some time in prayer reflecting on this week's lessons. Ask God to speak to your heart and reveal to you what's important. Then spend some time answering the questions below. Write down your responses to discuss them in your small groups or as a journal entry to remember what you have learned.

INSIGHTS:

What are some of the key insights you have learned from this week's lessons? What has stood out to you? What has spoken to your heart?

Lesson 3 • Abundant Change

Lesson 4 • Abundant Newness

Lesson 5 • Abundant Worth

APPLICATIONS:

How should you respond to what you have learned in this week's lessons? What do you need to do differently? What changes do you feel the Lord leading you to make? What specific steps can you take?

See videos & more
under resources at
abundantlifestudy.com

55

ABUNDANT WEALTH
The Riches of Grace

—≪≪≪≪—

I pray also that the eyes of your heart may be
enlightened in order that you may know the hope
to which he has called you, the riches of his
glorious inheritance in the saints.
Ephesians 1:18 NIV

This lesson will continue to study the amazing benefits of salvation in Jesus Christ. God has done so much more than just forgive our sins. He has made us abundantly rich in Christ!

VERSES TO READ, STUDY, AND MEDITATE ON:

1. **God has given you every spiritual blessing**. God has not given you one or just a few of His spiritual blessings but every single one of them. This encompasses everything that you have studied so far and a lot of what you will continue to study in later lessons. This is an abundance of spiritual blessings beyond comprehension! It is important to emphasize here that the blessings are spiritual, not material. This means they are available to every single Christian, no matter where they live or what their circumstances. *Ephesians 1:3, 1:18, 3:8;* then read all of *Ephesians chapters 1 and 2.* Many of the spiritual blessings follow from verse 1:3 onward.

See videos & more
under resources at
abundantlifestudy.com

2. **God has given you an inheritance.** You are joint heirs with Christ. You are studying many of the riches of your inheritance that God has given you now. There are many others that await you in Heaven that you have either already studied or will cover in later lessons. You could study these for the rest of your life, because they are so numerous and deep! *Romans 8:17; Ephesians 1:14-18; 1 Peter 1:3-5 (Galatians 3:29; Hebrews 9:15; Titus 3:7)*

3. **God has given you unlimited access.** You can go to God in prayer anytime and anywhere. He is always ready to listen and help you according to His will. You have the incredible privilege to talk with the almighty God who created the entire universe. He is everywhere (omnipresent), knows all things (omniscient), and is all powerful (omnipotent). He invites you to come as a child of God to the Father, your new spiritual and eternal Father. Children have access to their Father. *Romans 5:1-2; Ephesians 2:17-18, 3:12; Hebrews 4:16 (Romans 8:15)*

4. **God has promised to meet all of your needs.** God will meet all of your genuine needs to accomplish His will and plan for your life. People often want more than they need. This promise should begin to provide freedom from worry (this will be discussed later). *Philippians 4:19; Luke 12:22-31 (Romans 8:32)*

5. **God has given you fellowship.** God has given you fellowship with Himself and with other believers in Christ. You are part of God's family and can enjoy the company of God and each other every day. Do not forget that God dwells within you for constant fellowship if you seek Him and depend upon Him. You are never alone! *Psalm 139; 1 Corinthians 1:9; 1 John 1:1-7; Philippians 2:1 (Acts 2:42)*

6. **God has given you the Holy Spirit to dwell in you.** This has already been studied, but it is an incomprehensible fact that you should meditate on every day. God lives within you! The riches and blessings that come from the Holy Spirit will be covered throughout this study. *Ephesians 1:13-14; 2 Timothy 1:14; 1 John 4:13 (John 17:20-26; Romans 8:9-11; Galatians 2:20-21; Colossians 1:27)*

7. **God has given you eternal life now.** Eternal life, which is also a new quality of life, does not start when you die but the moment you are saved. Eternal life starts right now, here on earth, so that you know that you are saved and headed to Heaven. In *John 17:3* Jesus defines eternal life as knowing God in a personal, interactive, and experiential relationship. This is tremendously encouraging and exciting! *John 5:24, 10:28, 11:25-26, 17:1-3; 1 John 5:11-13*

8. **God has given you His Word.** The Bible is the Word of God. It is His revelation to mankind of who He is, what He is like, and His plan of salvation in Jesus Christ. In our modern age, we often overlook the tremendous blessing and responsibility it is to have His complete Word. It is essential to the Christian life. It is alive and has power that no other words in any book have. Jesus Christ is called the Word of God. You cannot know Jesus if you do not know the Word of God (Bible). (For an in-depth study of incredible validation of the Bible see The God Diagnosis by Dr. Greg Viehman.) *John 1:1-3; 2 Timothy 3:16-17; Hebrews 4:12-13; 2 Peter 1:16-21 (Psalm 119)*

9. **God has given you knowledge and wisdom in Jesus.** Jesus is your wisdom. He lives in you and guides your life. Jesus is the living, incarnate Word of God. The Word provides you wisdom and knowledge for daily life and about God and His plan for you. This is another reason to know and read the Bible all the time. *1 Corinthians 1:24; Colossians 2:1-10; 2 Peter 1:2-4*

See videos & more
under resources at
abundantlifestudy.com

QUESTIONS TO PONDER:

1. Read *Matthew 27:50-54* and *Luke 23:44-46*. During the death of Jesus Christ on the cross, the veil in the temple, which separated the people from God's presence, was torn from top to bottom. This was a huge and very large cloth barrier to God's presence. What was God proclaiming? What does torn from top to bottom imply?

2. Read *2 Timothy 3:16-17*. List and discuss the benefits of the Word of God.

3. Read *Luke 12:13-21*. What does this story tell us about abundant material possessions?

4. OPTIONAL: Read *Psalm 119*. Make a list of all the benefits from the Word of God that you can find. There are over 40! It is worth finding them.

See videos & more
under resources at
abundantlifestudy.com

WEEK 3 • LESSON 7
Abundant Power

ABUNDANT POWER
The Empowerment of Grace

—≪≪≪≪—

His divine power has given us everything we need
for life and godliness through our knowledge of
him who called us by his own glory and goodness.
2 Peter 1:3 NIV

The Christian life is filled with struggles and trials because we live in a fallen world. We also live in a fallen body that still has a sinful nature (or flesh), which is prone towards selfishness and sin. On top of that there is an enemy, Satan, and his demons who war against us. God intends, however, that despite these challenging circumstances of our existence, we will still have victory, not of ourselves but by the power of God. The Lord has given us the Holy Spirit and the power of God within us, and He also acts on our behalf in our circumstances.

God has given us access to His power to live a victorious Christian life, but we must work diligently to grow, mature, heal, train, and be strengthened. We must learn how to be used by Him through His power. All of these topics will be discussed in Part III of this study, but for now we only need to understand that power is available. We need to understand what is available, before we can be used by Him. If we do not know something is available how can we benefit from it?

See videos & more
under resources at
abundantlifestudy.com

VERSES TO READ, STUDY, AND MEDITATE ON:

1. **God has given you power for all aspects of the Christian life.** This is a general truth that encompasses many of the topics we will study. *Ephesians 1:15-21; 2 Peter 1:3-4*

2. **God has given you the power of the Holy Spirit.** The power and ministry of the Holy Spirit in the life of the believer will be examined throughout this study. The Holy Spirit gives you spiritual discernment over false teachings and situations requiring insight. This is also known in the Bible as the "anointing." He teaches you spiritual things. He also gives you spiritual gifts to empower your service for God and others, which is another study in itself. *John 14:26, 16:13; Romans 8:26-27; Ephesians 3:16-21; 2 Timothy 1:7; 1 John 2:20, 27 (Luke 12:12; Romans 12:3-8; Ephesians 4:7-16)*

3. **God has given you power over sin and the sinful nature/flesh.** This comes from the power of the Holy Spirit in you. The caveat is that you must grow and submit to the Holy Spirit in order to realize this power and find victory. This will be covered in Part III. God has also broken the power of sin over you, which will be covered in the next lesson. *Romans 8:1-17, 13:14; Galatians 5:16-25; Hebrews 2:18; 2 Peter 1:3-4*

4. **God has given you power for trials and struggles in life.** The Christian life is filled with trials and struggles. God has given you His power to persevere and even find great joy and hope through life's difficulties. *Isaiah 41:10; 2 Corinthians 4:7-11, 12:7-10, 13:4; Philippians 3:10-11, 4:11-13; Colossians 1:10-13; 2 Timothy 1:8-12*

5. **God has given you power to love God and others.** Loving God and others are the two great commandments. The problem is that we do not have in ourselves the kind of love that God wants us to show. The Greek word for this love is agape, which means an unselfish and sacrificial love that is focused on others rather than on ourselves. You do not have this love instinctively since it only comes from God. He gives it to you by the power of the Holy Spirit. *Romans 5:5; 2 Timothy 1:7*

6. **God has given you power to do His will.** God has given you divine enablement when you are serving Him and working to accomplish His will. You have the power of prayer from both the Holy Spirit and Jesus Himself working for you! *Romans 8:26-27, 34; Philippians 2:13; Hebrews 13:20-21; 2 Timothy 4:17*

7. **God has given you power to resist the devil.** God has given you the armor of God, but you must know that you have it and what the different parts of the armor are used for. You also have to put it on daily. This will be covered in Part III. *2 Corinthians 10:3-6; Ephesians 6:10-18; James 4:7-10; 1 Peter 5:8-11 (Revelation 12:9-11)*

8. **God has given you the power of the Word of God.** The Word of God is living and able to do a plethora of things for the Christian who will continue to read and study it. As you will learn in future lessons, it is essential for Christian growth, love, transformation, and victory. *Psalm 119:11; Jeremiah 23:29; Ephesians 6:17; 1 Thessalonians 2:13; 2 Timothy 3:16-17; Hebrews 4:12*

9. **God has given you the power of His joy and peace.** Joy is an unselfish internal happiness that comes from God and is not dependent upon external circumstances. God's peace is an internal quietness, serenity, and satisfaction of the spirit/soul which is at rest because of God's love and presence. Joy and peace are powerful, especially when you are facing life's trials. A state of internal joy and peace empowers you to focus on others, since people are not instinctively striving to obtain that state. Before people are saved, many spend their time pursuing internal joy and peace from things that can never deliver them. *Nehemiah 8:10; John 14:27, 16:33; Romans 15:13; Philippians 4:4-9; 2 Thessalonians 3:16 (John 20:19-23; Galatians 5:22)*

10. **God keeps you by His power.** A Christian's salvation, eternity in Heaven, and life here on earth are secured by the power of God. This is not a guarantee that you will not have problems, because you will. Rest assured, however, that God is in control. *John 17:15; 2 Timothy 1:12; 1 Peter 1:4-5; Jude 24-25*

See videos & more under resources at abundantlifestudy.com

QUESTIONS TO PONDER:

1. Read *2 Timothy 1:7*, *Ephesians 3:14-21*, and *Philippians 4:13*. How is the Holy Spirit living within you a source of power? What can He empower you to do that you cannot do on your own? How can God strengthen you?

2. Read *2 Timothy 3:16-17*, *Ephesians 6:17*, and *Hebrews 4:12*. How is the Word of God a source of power for the Christian? When you look at your Bible, do you see it as a source of power? Do you think this power is underappreciated and underutilized? Why?

3. Read *Matthew 22:34-40*, *John 15:9-17*, and *1 Corinthians 13:1-13*. Why is God's power to love Him and others so essential to the Christian life?

See videos & more
under resources at
abundantlifestudy.com

ABUNDANT FREEDOM
The Liberty of Grace

─≪≪≪─

If you abide in My word, you are My disciples
indeed. And you shall know the truth,
and the truth shall make you free.
John 8:31-32 NKJV

The abundant life is a life of freedom! Jesus came to set us free, but we need to abide or live in His Word (the Bible). Why? Because all of the truths that will set us free are in the Word of God. When we read the Bible and learn truth, it is not just an intellectual exercise, but the Word does a spiritual surgery in our hearts. This is exactly why we are spending so much time looking up and reading Scripture. The pathway to freedom is to abide in the Word, know the truth, obey the truths you discover, and then let the truth set you free. We have been doing this all along and are being set free right now as we complete this study. We have already learned a lot of truth, and there is much more to come. Abundant freedom is ours, thanks to Jesus!

VERSES TO READ, STUDY, AND MEDITATE ON:

1. **Freedom from the penalty of sin.** The penalty for sin is death (*Romans 6:23*)—separation from God. We were born separated and will remain separated from God (in hell) after physical death if we are not saved. Jesus Christ died in your place and took the death penalty for you. When you were saved, you were freed from the death penalty of sin. Your sins are forgiven and forgotten, as you have studied. You will go to Heaven and not hell. *John 11:25-26; Romans 5:1-2, 6:23; Colossians 2:13-15*

See videos & more
under resources at
abundantlifestudy.com

2. **Freedom from the bondage and power of sin.** Jesus Christ broke the power of sin by His victory on the cross. A combination of the Holy Spirit living within a person and being a new person with a new heart and mind provides power over sin that the person did not have before salvation. There is a new ability to say no to sin and live a new life according to God's will. Before a person is saved, he or she is dead in sin and controlled by it, but after salvation the person is dead to sin and does not have to be controlled by it. In Part III you will learn how to fully realize this victory in your life. A key step in victory over sin is knowing that it no longer has power over you. Knowledge is power. *Romans chapter 6, 8:1-4; John 8:31-36; Galatians 5:16-26*

3. **Freedom from the preoccupation of sin.** A Christian gets all of their righteousness before God from Jesus Christ, as you have already studied. You do not earn righteousness by good behavior or lose it by bad behavior (sin). You therefore do not have to focus on keeping a list of rules to be righteous and accepted before God. You are already declared righteous and accepted in Christ. As you will learn later, if you focus on Christ and His Word, the Holy Spirit will naturally empower you to do what is right and avoid what is wrong without the preoccupation of rules and regulations. Some Christians think they are in a higher level of acceptance before God because of what they do and do not do, compared to others. There are no elite levels of righteousness or acceptance. You are free from this bondage! *Romans chapter 7; Galatians 5:1-6; Colossians 2:16-23; 2 Timothy 1:9*

4. **Freedom from the condemnation of sin.** There is no condemnation from God because of sin for the saved Christian. Sin will bring death, misery, and its own consequences into even a Christian's life, but there is no condemnation, because we are in Christ. This truth sets your conscience free of past guilt and failures. Guilt stifles the truth that God loves you and diminishes your desire to seek God and obey Him. You need to be free from guilt and condemnation of sin before you can fully deal with the current presence of sin in your life. *Romans 8:1; Psalm 103:12*

5. **Freedom from inadequacy, inferiority, and insecurity.** Your abundant worth, wealth, newness, and change (that you have already studied) all

combine to set you free from these three menaces in life. Your position in Christ gives you acceptance, belonging, forgiveness, and a fresh start as a new creation which frees you from feeling insecure. Who you are in Christ (your person in Christ) as a son, ambassador, priest, temple, etc., frees you from feeling inferior because you have such abundant worthiness by God's grace. Finally, your abundant wealth or possessions in Christ free you from feeling inadequate because you have abundant power, blessings, and promises from God that give you competence and confidence in Him. Review these lessons briefly in this new context. *Romans 8:29-39; Colossians 2:9-10. See also Lessons 4, 5, and 6.*

6. **Freedom from fear, anxiety, and worry.** Fear and anxiety often come from the unknown. You may worry about what might happen and fear what you cannot control. You probably worry about money and having what you need in life. God, however, is in control and promises that all things work for your good, that He will meet all of your genuine needs, and that He will help you in your time of need. He will also actively guard your heart and mind with His love, joy, and peace if you pray to Him and meditate on these promises. *Isaiah 41:10; Luke 12:22-34; Romans 8:28-39; Philippians 4:4-7; 1 John 4:18*

7. **Freedom from depression.** There are two basic forms of depression: spiritual and physical (or medical). There are clearly disease states that cause depression from chemical imbalances in the brain that are not related to life's circumstances or spiritual influences. In my professional opinion, however, the vast majority of cases are spiritual in origin. A lot of depression derives from being separated from God and trying to be fulfilled in life apart from God. People are empty and lonely without their Creator, with whom they were created to have a relationship. People also get down about the past, present, and future. Jesus has the cure for depression by reconciling you to God and ending the separation. He also took care of your past, present, and future sins and failures. He will be with you in your present trials, and He promises that all things work for your good. Your future ends with eternal life in Heaven no matter what happens here on earth. The power of His joy, which you have already studied, is a powerful antidote for depression. *Nehemiah 8:10; John 15:11; Romans chapter 8*

8. **Freedom from death.** We are all physically dying. Many people fear death because it is an unknown. A Christian does not have to fear physical death because when you die you go straight into the arms of Jesus. Death is not the end but, rather, the beginning of eternity in God's presence. Even more, you will never die spiritually (be separated from God) but have eternal life even right now. *John 3:16, 10:27-30; Acts 7:54-60; 1 Corinthians 15:53-56; 2 Corinthians 5:1-8; Philippians 1:21-26*

9. **Freedom from the world.** The "world" is not the physical world of nature but the entire system of fallen human existence that is opposed to the true and living God and His cure for the salvation from sin. It is ruled by Satan and targets the sinful nature/flesh through lust and pride as a means for self-fulfillment and self-preservation. Remember, you are not of this world, but are supposed to be a light in it! Jesus has overcome the world and so can you through Him. *John 16:33; Colossians 2:8, 20-23; 2 Peter 1:2-4; 1 John 2:15-17, 5:4-5 (Matthew 5:14-16; John 17:14-19; Galatians 6:14; James 1:27)*

QUESTIONS TO PONDER:

1. Read *Romans chapter 6*. Underline every time the word "dead," "died," "death," or any reference to death is used. Count how many times this occurs in this chapter. What is Paul trying to tell you and emphasize in this chapter?

2. Read *Romans 6:3* and *6:16*. Notice that Paul asks, "Don't you know...?" After each question he then states what you should know. He uses the word "knowing" again in verses *6:6* and *6:9*. What does he want you to know? Why is this so critical to the abundant Christian life? Discuss how knowledge is power. In Part III of the study you will learn how to apply this knowledge for victory over sin, but you first have to "know."

3. How does everything you have learned so far help to set you free from inadequacy, inferiority, insecurity, depression, and anxiety?

See videos & more under resources at abundantlifestudy.com

REFLECTIONS
Week 3

Spend some time in prayer reflecting on this week's lessons. Ask God to speak to your heart and reveal to you what's important. Then spend some time answering the questions below. Write down your responses to discuss them in your small groups or as a journal entry to remember what you have learned.

INSIGHTS:

What are some of the key insights you have learned from this week's lessons? What has stood out to you? What has spoken to your heart?

Lesson 6 • Abundant Wealth

Lesson 7 • Abundant Power

Lesson 8 • Abundant Freedom

APPLICATIONS:

How should you respond to what you have learned in this week's lessons? What do you need to do differently? What changes do you feel the Lord leading you to make? What specific steps can you take?

See videos & more
under resources at
abundantlifestudy.com

ABUNDANT SECURITY
The Safety of Grace

─‹‹‹‹‹‹

*"My sheep hear My voice, and I know them,
and they follow Me. And I give them eternal life,
and they shall never perish; neither shall anyone
snatch them out of My hand. My Father, who has
given them to Me, is greater than all; and no one is
able to snatch them out of My Father's hand.
I and My Father are one."*
John 10:27-30 NKJV

We have already studied the price that Jesus paid for our sins (Lesson 1) and the amazing results of the salvation that He purchased (Lessons 2-8). Salvation is an eternal and irreversible transaction. When a person is saved by God's grace through faith they are eternally secure and kept by the power of God's sovereignty. The transactions and radical changes to the nature of our existence that occur at the moment of salvation forever secure our eternal destiny as a child of God. This is an absolutely critical gift from God that we need to understand and believe in order to be truly free from fear and death. It is a major source of fuel to empower a relationship with God based upon gratitude and love. To know that you are forever secure in Christ right now here on earth in this fallen world is one of God's greatest gifts to His children. It invaluably kindles joy, peace, gratitude, faith, hope, and love in our hearts.

See videos & more
under resources at
abundantlifestudy.com

VERSES TO READ, STUDY, AND MEDITATE ON:

1. **Eternal Life.** Eternal life means forever. Forever is forever. Eternal is eternal. Although this is basic common sense, it is often overlooked. God says that you have eternal life when you are saved. This means you will live forever and never perish or lose your salvation. Not one verse in the Bible ever says eternal life "until".... Remember, eternal life starts the day a person is saved! You possess eternal life right now if you are in Christ. Eternal life is not simply existing forever but living a new quality of life because God lives in you and you have a relationship with Him. *John 3:15-16, 8:35-36, 10:27-30; Romans 6:23; Titus 3:4-7; 1 John 2:17, 25*

2. **Eternal Security.** This is the obvious natural result of the verses above. You are eternally secure in Jesus Christ. You cannot lose your salvation by sin or bad behavior. When a person is saved he or she is in Christ with all of the person's sins forgiven, forgotten, and paid for by the blood of Jesus Christ (see Lesson 3). Jesus paid for all of your sin before you were born. If you could lose your salvation, then there is a sin that Jesus did not pay for. If you could lose your salvation, then what Jesus did on the cross is not sufficient to save you and keep you. In contrast, God says you are kept eternally secure by the power of God. If a person is saved, then God sees that person as already glorified with Him in Heaven. *Romans 8:29-30, 35-39; John 6:39-40, 10:27-30, 11:25-26; 1 Peter 1:3-5*

3. **Present Certainty.** Because eternal security is so liberating and makes you want to praise and serve God from gratitude, God wants you to be certain of this precious gift right now. Jesus wants you to know that you are His sheep with eternal life that no one can take away. This certainty comes from God living within you and from growing and maturing in your faith, which you will study in Part III. This is a strong incentive to know and grow! *Romans 8:15-16; 2 Corinthians 5:5; Galatians 4:6; Philippians 1:19-26; 1 John 4:13, 5:13*

4. **Sealed with the Holy Spirit.** God says that when He saves a person he or she is indwelt and sealed by the Holy Spirit forever. A seal in biblical times was a mark of ownership and security. This seal is called

a down payment or promise until you go to Heaven permanently. God put His Holy Spirit in you so you know you belong to Him and are secure in Him. You are personally "sealed" by God as His own, which no one can touch but Him. *Ephesians 1:13-14, 4:30; 2 Corinthians 1:22 (John 14:16)*

5. **Irreversibly Changed and Transformed.** In Lesson 4 you learned that, as a result of salvation in Jesus Christ, you are born again as a new person with a new heart and mind into the family of God. You are a new creation in Christ. These analogies confirm the permanence and security of salvation. Can a person be unborn? Can a new creation, like a butterfly, revert back to the old caterpillar? If your old man died, then does he get resurrected so you can lose your salvation? If God adopts you into His family, does He disown you as His child because of sin? Is that the kind of God who died upon the cross to save you? Is that the kind of salvation that Jesus purchased on the cross? Did the God-man die for the sins of the world so that He could disown you at His discretion? No! *John 3:3,16-17; Romans 6:5-10, 8:15-16; 2 Corinthians 5:17; 1 Peter 1:3*

6. **Saved by Grace.** The Bible is clear that you are saved by grace through faith and NOT by your good works. If anything is added to the free gift of grace, it is no longer grace. If you can lose your salvation, then there is something you can do or not do to keep it. This, then, makes salvation dependent upon your obedience and performance, which is not grace. By definition, salvation by grace ensures that it is permanent. *Galatians 2:16-21; Ephesians 2:8-9; Titus 3:4-7, 11:6 (Romans 3:20, chapter 4; 2 Timothy 1:9)*

There are a few important rules of Bible interpretation that are important to emphasize here:

When the simple sense of a verse makes common sense, then seek no other sense or you will make nonsense. In other words, when a verse is plain and clear in what it says, then that is what it means. Do not look for another meaning because it does not fit your own personal theology. God says what He means and means what He says.

See videos & more under resources at abundantlifestudy.com

Scripture interprets Scripture. There is a harmony in the Word of God. Do not let a single verse or a few obscure verses become a source of doctrine if they do not seem to fit with the rest of the Bible. God makes the important and major points very clear so you are not confused.

The verses that are plain and clear for major important doctrines take precedence over obscure and harder to understand verses. This is especially important here because there are a lot of Christian groups that falsely teach that you can lose your salvation. The common denominator is that they will show you verses that do not speak clearly about salvation and seem to suggest you can lose it. Although you may not always fully understand what these verses mean, they never override the many verses that you have just studied that plainly and emphatically teach eternal security. God has made it clear that you are secure in Christ. All verses must be read in their immediate context, and the larger context of the entire book they appear in, and the entire Bible. Most verses that are used to cause confusion about eternal security are taken out of context. Read the surrounding sentences and paragraphs to determine the context of a single verse.

Never build a doctrine on one verse or a few obscure verses. Be sure to include other verses that address your topic and properly support it from the context. Every verse must be read and understood in its original context.

QUESTIONS TO PONDER:

1. Read *2 Samuel chapters 11* and *12*. David committed adultery, lied, coveted, stole, and murdered. The Bible is clear that David is a man of God and will have a special place in the coming Kingdom. In *Romans chapter 4*, he is used as an example of salvation by grace through faith. Discuss how David is an example of salvation by grace through faith apart from his behavior. How many Christians have sinned as badly as David did? How could David still go to Heaven after all of these sins? Did David get away without paying the price? Discuss how consequences are not an indication of rejection.

2. Read also: *2 Samuel chapter 7; Romans 4:5-8.* How do these verses contribute to your understanding of salvation?

3. Read *John 10:27-30.* Discuss how this Scripture clearly teaches eternal security. How does Jesus emphasize this in several different ways?

4. Discuss how the various analogies that God has chosen to describe salvation teach eternal security: born again, adopted, new creation, the old man has died, sealed with the Holy Spirit. Discuss how understanding what happens at salvation and how you are saved secures your salvation and refutes the false teaching that you can lose it.

5. Read *Galatians 2:20-21.* If there are things you must do or not do to maintain and keep your salvation, then what does this say about what Jesus did on the cross to save you?

See videos & more under resources at abundantlifestudy.com

ABUNDANT HOPE
The Certainty of Grace

—≪≪≪—

*Now may the God of hope fill you with all joy and
peace in believing, that you may abound in hope
by the power of the Holy Spirit.*
Romans 15:13 NKJV

Hope for the Christian is a certainty of good things to come. It is not an uncertain desire based upon wishful thinking such as "I hope I get that new job." Biblical hope is a certainty of good things to come which include Heaven, eternal life, resurrection, a new glorified body, and all the promises of God. True hope in the heart is empowering, protective, and loving.

VERSES TO READ, STUDY, AND MEDITATE ON:

1. **Heavenly Hope.** Heaven is a real place where you will be in the presence of God's glory. It will be perfect and you will be made perfect. The hope of Heaven is certain and powerful. You are a citizen of Heaven and headed home one day in God's timing. Your hope is in Heaven. *Romans 5:1-5; Ephesians 1:18; Philippians 3:20; Colossians 1:3-5; Revelation 21:1-8 (Luke 10:20)*

2. **Eternal Hope.** Eternal life is something that you possess right now. Having eternal life is knowing God in a personal relationship that will last forever. You will never die or be separated from Him. When we die physically we will enter into the eternal life that we already possess

right now. Physical death is the door to eternity. You have part of your hope right now. (This topic was covered in detail in Lesson 9.) *Mark 10:30; John 10:27-30, 17:1-3; Romans 6:23; Titus 1:1-3, 3:4-7 (Matthew 25:46; John 3:15-16)*

3. **Resurrection Hope.** The resurrection is the hope of Christianity and is based upon the bodily resurrection of Jesus Christ as a genuine historical event in time. Right now, we live in fallen, sin-tainted bodies that are slowly, physically dying and decaying, but at the resurrection we will receive glorified bodies like Jesus. Your glorified body will be perfect. Jesus in His glorified body could eat, be touched, and was a real person with His same identity. You have the hope of a new body that is perfect and made by God to forever be in His presence in Heaven. *Romans 8:23-25, 29-30; 1 Corinthians 15:12-23, 35-58; Philippians 3:20-21; 1 John 1:1-4, 3:2 (Acts 23:6)*

4. **Internal Hope.** The hope of Jesus Christ lives within you. It is not merely an intellectual fact that we embrace but a living reality within our existence. The Holy Spirit who lives inside of you empowers and manifests the hope of salvation in your heart. It is a gift from God. *Romans 5:5, 15:13; Colossians 1:27; 1 Peter 3:15*

5. **Living Hope.** Your hope is in the living Savior Jesus Christ. He is the God-man who has been resurrected from the dead and is forever alive. Christians await His return and His final redemption of our bodies. This is a living hope based upon a living Savior who is the eternal God and the author of everything living. *1 Timothy 1:1; Titus 2:13; 1 Peter 1:3-4, 21; 1 John 1:1-4*

6. **Purifying Hope.** The hope of receiving a glorified body and becoming like the Lord motivates believers to purify themselves. The certainty of this awesome day coming creates a desire to turn away from sin and seek to be more like Jesus. *1 John 3:1-3; 2 Corinthians 7:1*

7. **Anchoring Hope.** God always keeps His promises. The living hope of salvation and eternity in Heaven in a glorified body is an anchor for your soul. It holds you in the right place and keeps you from drifting according to the wind or currents of this world. It keeps you secure in

the stormy waters of this world. Jesus has a heavenly anchor attached to you. *Hebrews 6:19*

8. **Joyful Hope.** Your hope is linked to joy. Joy is an internal state of delight, elation, and satisfaction that comes from God and is independent of external circumstances. Your hope is so awesome, tangible, and experiential that it should cause great joy. You are eternally saved and have eternal life right now living within you. You have a one way ticket home to Heaven where you will have a glorified body and forever be with your Savior. Think about this! As a Christian, how can this create anything but intense joy? *Psalm 16:9-11; Romans 12:12, 15:13; 1 John 1:1-4; Philippians 3:1, 4:4*

9. **Loving Hope.** Faith, hope, and love appear a lot together in the Scriptures. Faith fosters hope and hope stimulates love. When you have a certainty of God's hope within you, then you are free to love others and stop focusing on yourself. God's love poured into your heart by the Holy Spirit also strengthens and affirms your hope. Hope loves and love hopes. *1 Corinthians 13:13; Romans 5:5*

10. **Patient Hope.** Hope produces patience. When you are certain of your destiny and have living hope inside of you, you are strengthened to endure difficult situations. You can look forward to Heaven and what you know is coming and endure. No matter what happens to you in this life, you have eternal life and Heaven awaiting. *Psalm 62:5, 130:5; Romans 5:1-5, 8:18-25; Galatians 5:5; 1 Thessalonians 1:3*

11. **Protective Hope.** Hope can protect your mind. Having a certainty of eternal life now and all the promises of Heaven, is protective for your mind. The Bible refers to the "helmet of salvation," and it is our salvation that is the foundation of our hope. Having an eternal perspective and paradigm of life, which is your reality, will protect you from the flesh and from sin, depression, discouragement, worldly pursuits, fear, and many other problems that emanate from a godless worldview. Hope is armor for your mind. *Ephesians 6:17; Colossians 3:1-4; 1 Thessalonians 5:8-11*

See videos & more under resources at abundantlifestudy.com

QUESTIONS TO PONDER:

1. Read *1 John 1:1-4* and *3:1-3*. What is the hope John is talking about? Why and how does this lead to purification? What should hope encourage you to do that results in purification?

2. Read *Romans 8:18-25*. What is the hope we are waiting for? Why and how should it result in patience?

3. Read *Luke chapter 24*, *Philippians 3:20-21*, and *1 John 3:2-3*. What was Jesus like after the resurrection? What does this tell you about what you will be like? How should this nurture a tremendous sense of hope within you? List and discuss as many things as you can find.

See videos & more
under resources at
abundantlifestudy.com

ABUNDANT PLANS
The Details of Grace

—≪≪≪≪

For we are His workmanship, created in Christ Jesus for good works, which God prepared beforehand that we should walk in them.
Ephesians 2:10 NKJV

God has an amazing personal plan for our lives which is designed to bring Him glory and transform us into the image of Jesus Christ. The eternal almighty God has a detailed plan and purpose for our lives where He promises to guide us through. He will fulfill if we will obey and follow Him. This plan is the reason that we were created, and there is no true meaning or fulfillment in life apart from it. As we shall see in later lessons, this is a very compelling reason to walk in the Lord's will.

VERSES TO READ, STUDY, AND MEDITATE ON:

1. **Abundant Thoughts.** God says He thinks about you more than you can comprehend. He cares about you and the details of your life. He is thinking about you and desiring to see you fulfill His plan for your life. *Psalm 40:5, 139:17-18; Isaiah 55:8-9*

2. **Abundant Details.** God's thoughts and plans for your life are detailed. He has a specific career and pathway where He wants each of us to walk in the power of the Holy Spirit. His plans were in place before you were born. *Psalm 139:13-16; Jeremiah 1:5, 29:11-13; Ephesians 1:1, 2:10 (Colossians 1:1; 2 Timothy 1:9)*

See videos & more under resources at abundantlifestudy.com

3. **Abundant Preparation.** God is preparing a place for us in heaven that is specifically designed for each and every one of us. He has also made preparation for you to walk in His will and plans. *John 14:1-3; Ephesians 2:10; Philippians 1:6, 2:12-13*

4. **Abundant Goodness.** God has promised that all of His plans are good for you even if you do not understand them at the moment you are experiencing them. All things work for your good if you are trying to walk in His will and obey Him (loving God). *Genesis 50:20; Jeremiah 29:11; Romans 8:28*

5. **Abundant Guidance.** God promises to guide you through His plan for your life. If God is for you, who can be against you? He is with you at all times. *Psalm 32:8, 57:2, 73:23-24, 138:8; Proverbs 3:5-6, 16:3, 16:9; Matthew 28:20; John 16:13; Romans 8:31 (Isaiah 58:11)*

6. **Abundant Transformation.** God intends to transform and mold you into the likeness of Jesus (sanctification). He wants you to surrender to Him so He can renew your mind and clean you up from the inside out. This is God's will and plan for you. *Romans 8:29-30, 12:1-2; 2 Corinthians 3:18; 1 Thessalonians 4:3*

7. **Abundant Fruit.** The result of your transformation is bearing the fruit of agape love. God intends for you to show His love to Him and others. (This will be discussed in detail in Part III.) *John 15:1-8, 16; Galatians 5:22-23*

8. **Abundant Joy, Prayer, and Thanks.** God desires for you to be filled with joy and to be very thankful. He wants you to communicate with Him through prayer. *Psalm 34:1; Romans 12:12, 15:13; 1 Thessalonians 5:16-18; Ephesians 5:17-20; Philippians 4:4; Colossians 3:17, 4:2; Hebrews 13:15*

9. **Abundant Glory.** Your purpose in life is to glorify God. This is His plan and purpose for you. If you walk in His plan, you will bring Him glory. *Matthew 5:16; John 15:8; 1 Corinthians 6:19-20, 10:31*

QUESTIONS TO PONDER:

WEEK 4 • LESSON 11
Abundant Plans

1. If God has such abundant plans, preparation, and goodness for your life that will glorify Him and change you, then how do you discover and walk in His plan? Your answers will help prepare you for Parts II and III of this study.

2. Read *Psalm 139*. What can you learn about God and His plan for your life from this psalm?

3. Read *Colossians 1:1* and *Ephesians 1:1*. Paul said He was an apostle by the will of God. What are you by the will of God? Do you know? Are you certain? God wants you to know this with all of your heart. If you do not know, then you are on the path to finding out! There is nothing more joyous and gratifying than to know God's purpose for your life and watching Him fulfill it.

REFLECTIONS
Week 4

Spend some time in prayer reflecting on this week's lessons. Ask God to speak to your heart and reveal to you what's important. Then spend some time answering the questions below. Write down your responses to discuss them in your small groups or as a journal entry to remember what you have learned.

INSIGHTS:

What are some of the key insights you have learned from this week's lessons? What has stood out to you? What has spoken to your heart?

Lesson 9 • Abundant Security

Lesson 10 • Abundant Hope

Lesson 11 • Abundant Plans

APPLICATIONS:

How should you respond to what you have learned in this week's lessons? What do you need to do differently? What changes do you feel the Lord leading you to make? What specific steps can you take?

See videos & more under resources at abundantlifestudy.com

PART I SUMMARY
Abundant Revelation: Grace

Before Salvation	After Salvation
Old man alive	Old man dead New man created/new creation in Christ
Born sinful	Born again of God
Created in sin	Created anew in righteousness and holiness
Spiritually dead (separated from God)	Spiritually alive (connected to God)
Spiritually deaf	Spiritual hearing
Spiritually blind	Spiritual vision
No Holy Spirit in you	Holy Spirit in you
Slave to sin	Slave to God
No hope	Hope of Heaven and eternal life
Unregenerate	Regenerated
Dead in sin	Dead to sin
No power over sin	Power over sin
Sins not forgiven	Sins forgiven and forgotten
Sinful/unrighteous standing with God	Righteous standing with God
Child of wrath/enemy of God	Child of God (adopted) / friend of God
Sinful heart	New heart
Reprobate mind	Mind of Christ
Headed to hell	Headed to Heaven

GOD HAS PROVIDED ABUNDANT

Change	Newness	Worth	Wealth	Power
Sins Forgiven and Forgotten Declared Righteous You Are In Christ Christ Is In You Redeemed Eternal Life Now Spiritually Alive Holy Spirit In You	Old Man Is Dead New Man Is Created New Birth New Creation New Heart New Mind New Relationship New Family New Citizenship	God's Workmanship God's Ambassador God's Child God's Temple God's Priest God's Saint Salt Of The Earth Light In The World Conformed To The Image Of Jesus God's Chosen Abundantly Loved More than a Conqueror Member Of The Body of Christ Bride of Christ	Every Spiritual Blessing An Inheritance In Christ Unlimited Access All Needs Met By God Fellowship Holy Spirit Of God In You Eternal Life Now The Word Of God Knowledge And Wisdom	For The Christian Life Of The Holy Spirit Over Sin and Sinful Nature For Trials and Struggles To Love God and Others To Do His Will To Resist The Devil Of The Word of God His Joy and Peace Kept By The Power Of God

Freedom	Security	Hope	Plans
Penalty Of Sin Bondage and Power Of Sin Preoccupation Of Sin Condemnation Of Sin Inadequacy, Inferiority, and Insecurity Fear, Anxiety, and Worry Depression Death The World	Eternal Life Eternal Security Present Certainty Sealed By The Holy Spirit Irreversibly Changed and Transformed Saved By Grace	Heavenly Hope Eternal Hope Resurrection Hope Internal Hope Living Hope Purifying Hope Anchoring Hope Joyful Hope Loving Hope Patient Hope Protective Hope	Abundant Thoughts Abundant Details Abundant Preparation Abundant Goodness Abundant Guidance Abundant Transformation Abundant Fruit Abundant Joy, Prayer, and Thanks Abundant Glory

PART II
ABUNDANT RESPONSE
Abundant Relationship

WEEK 5

LESSON 12 • **ABUNDANT SURRENDER:** THE DISCOVERY OF RELATIONSHIP

LESSON 13 • **ABUNDANT PRAISE:** THE GRATITUDE OF RELATIONSHIP

LESSON 14 • **ABUNDANT WORDS:** THE COMMUNICATION OF RELATIONSHIP

WEEK 6

LESSON 15 • **ABUNDANT GOD:** THE INTERACTION OF RELATIONSHIP

LESSON 16 • **ABUNDANT REPENTANCE:** THE CONVICTION OF RELATIONSHIP

LESSON 17 • **ABUNDANT LOVE FOR GOD:** THE HEART OF RELATIONSHIP

LESSON 18 • **ABUNDANT HEALTH:** THE WELLNESS OF RELATIONSHIP

THE HEALTHY HEART & HEART EXAMINATION

ABUNDANT SURRENDER
The Discovery of Relationship

—≪≪≪≪≪—

*Therefore, I urge you, brothers, in view of God's
mercy, to offer your bodies as living sacrifices,
holy and pleasing to God—this is your
spiritual act of worship.*
Romans 12:1 NIV

What should our response be after all that we have just studied in Part I? We have seen the depth of our depravity and the need for grace. We then learned about God's plan to save us, which is the rescue of grace. Finally, for several lessons we studied the results of salvation by grace. This revealed the infinite and unsearchable love, mercy, and grace of God. God's abundant revelation should create and motivate an abundant response on our part.

Knowing who God is, what He is like, and what He has done for us cannot help but generate an abundant response to God. The key and quintessential step in this response is surrender. God's abundant love, provision, power, and plans should bring us to our knees to know Him, obey Him, and follow His plan for our lives. Abundant gratitude, awe, wonder, and excitement should fill and compel our hearts to be consumed with the Lord. This is a personal commitment to let God etch our hearts with His will and plan for our lives to bring Him glory.

Surrender is giving our heart and lives back to God, who created us and saved us with His own life. Since He died for us, we should live for Him. Surrendering to the Lord is not giving up anything of importance but, instead, is discovering

See videos & more
under resources at
abundantlifestudy.com

God's eternal plan for our lives. It is dying to self so others might live, like Jesus did for us. Surrender is a daily process that is made voluntarily if we meditate on the truths of Part I. It is making God number one! Surrender is a process that matures. No one is ever fully surrendered at all times. Start where you can!

VERSES TO READ, STUDY, AND MEDITATE ON:

1. **Surrender your life.** Your life is your whole person, plans, and time. God has a plan for your entire life. Let Him show you what it is. Surrender your plans, schedule, and time to God! Make your time His time. This must be a daily commitment. *Matthew 16:24-27; Romans 6:16-23, 12:1-2; 2 Corinthians 5:14-15; Philippians 1:20-21 (Matthew 10:34-39; Romans 1:1; 2 Timothy 2:4)*

2. **Surrender your heart.** Your heart is the control system of your real spiritual person. It is the innermost part of your being. It consists of your will, emotions, conscience, and mental processes. Your desires, reasoning, and attitudes emanate from the heart. You need to allow God to empower and etch your heart with His will. *Deuteronomy 6:5-6; Psalm 37:4-5, 40:8, 119:36; Matthew 22:37-38; Luke 22:42; John 6:38, 28:9; James 4:7-8 (1 Chronicles 22:19; Ephesians 3:14-21)*

3. **Surrender your mind.** The mind is the center of your cognitive processes. You need God to establish your thoughts. You need your mind to be renewed, and this starts with surrender. *Psalm 37:5; Proverbs 16:3; Matthew 22:37-38; Romans 12:1-2; Colossians 3:1-3; Philippians 2:5-8 (1 Chronicles 28:9; Isaiah 26:3-4; Romans 8:5-8)*

4. **Surrender your possessions.** Everything belongs to God, including you. He owns and created everything. When you realize this, you should be grateful and willing to let Him use what He has given you for His purposes and glory. This is a state of the heart that understands where everything comes from and who really owns it. *Genesis 1:1; Deuteronomy 8:7-20; 1 Chronicles 29:11-12; Psalm 24:1-2; Isaiah 42:5, 44:24; James 1:17 (Psalm 50:10-12; Isaiah 45:18-19; Haggai 2:8)*

5. **Surrender in worship.** The heart of worship is surrender. It literally means to bow down. Worship sees what God is worth and gives Him what He is worth: all of your heart, mind, body, and soul. It is a state of the heart that—through faith—trusts, needs, and desires to know and praise God for who He is, what He is like, and what He has done in Jesus Christ. Worship is a state of awe, wonder, gratitude, need, trust, and praise that together culminate in a surrender of the heart and will to your Creator and Savior. *Psalm 29:2, 37:4, 96:9; John 4:21-24; Romans 12:1-2*

6. **Surrender from fear.** Fear of the Lord is not a trembling fear of danger, but a reverent respect for the awe and mighty wonder of God's person. It is an awareness of His sovereignty, omniscience, and omnipresence that stimulates your heart to surrender and creates a desire to obey His will and commands. This is a very healthy heart—it is very protective to have a reverent respect and honor for God that realizes He is God and you are not. *Proverbs 1:7, 9:10, 14:26-27, 15:33; Matthew 10:28 (Proverbs 1:29, 10:27, 14:2; Jeremiah 32:40-41)*

7. **Surrender from trust.** Surrender involves trust because you are entrusting all of your life and heart to God. You must trust Him with this. Trust is related to faith. *Proverbs 3:5; Psalm 9:10, 37:3-5, 118:8-9; Isaiah 26:3-4; 2 Corinthians 1:9-10*

8. **Surrender from need.** Jesus is your God and Savior. He gives you every breath and beat of your heart. You need God in order to accomplish anything for His will and glory. You need Him to empower your heart and keep you from sin. You still have a sinful nature/flesh that is selfish and opposed to the things of God and the Holy Spirit in you. You can win this war within you if you surrender. Surrender is a humble acknowledgement of great need and dependency that allows God to empower and show you His victory. You can intellectually acknowledge need but still trust in yourself. True surrender allows God to act and control. *Isaiah 42:5; John 15:1-8; Romans 7:13-25, 13:14; Galatians 5:16-25 (Acts 17:24-29; Philippians 4:13)*

See videos & more under resources at abundantlifestudy.com

9. **Surrender from desire.** Surrender involves a desire to acknowledge, thank, and know God because of what He has done and who He is. It involves seeking out the Lord's will by humbly coming to Him to guide your heart and mind. You should be eager and excited to come to Him, to learn His ways, and to understand His truths since they are delightful. *Deuteronomy 4:29; Psalm 1, 27, 40:8, 119:16, 35, 47; John 7:17; Philippians 3:7-11*

QUESTIONS TO PONDER:

1. Read *Romans 1:1, James 1:1, Jude 1:1, 2 Peter 1:1,* and *2 Timothy 2:4.* What do these men call themselves? Why? The Greek word is doulos or bondservant. Read *Deuteronomy 15:12-18.* What is a bondservant? Why would the apostles and disciples call themselves one? What can you learn about surrender from this?

2. Read *John 4:21-24.* What is the Father seeking? Why? What does worship "in spirit and truth" mean?

3. Read *Romans 12:1-2.* What is a living sacrifice? What is Paul asking you to do? He is making reference to the sacrificial system of the Old Testament. How does this give you an understanding of worship and surrender? What did Jesus do as the ultimate act of worship and surrender? In verse 2, what are the benefits of surrender?

4. In *1 Corinthians 15:31* Paul says, "I die every day." What important principle of surrender does Paul show you? Why is this necessary?

See videos & more
under resources at
abundantlifestudy.com

ABUNDANT PRAISE
The Gratitude of Relationship

—≪≪≪

Let everything that has breath praise the Lord. Praise the Lord!

Psalm 150:6 NKJV

Praise is a natural response emanating from a heart that is filled with the love, grace, mercy, and compassion of God. It is a state of the heart that is thanking God and expressing admiration and gratitude for salvation in Jesus Christ. Praise is a celebration of who God is, what He is like, and everything He has done for us (refer back to Part I). It is an outflow of surrender and worship that extols God's goodness and love and adores His majesty and holiness. Praise can be expressed in words or kept in the heart. When we meditate on the amazing grace, love, and mercy of God, as learned in Part I of this study, we cannot help but praise God. Abundant revelation causes abundant praise.

VERSES TO READ, STUDY, AND MEDITATE ON:

1. **He is God.** Praise Him for being God. *Exodus 15:2; Deuteronomy 10:21; Nehemiah 9:5-6; Psalm 34:1-3, 86:12-13, 146:1-2*

2. **He is worthy.** God is worthy of all praise. *2 Samuel 22:4; Psalm 9:1-2, 18:3, 48:1, 96:4-9, 113:3, 148:1-14, 150:1-6; Luke 19:37-40; Revelation 4:11, 5:11-13 (Psalm 96:4-9; 1 Thessalonians 5:18)*

See videos & more under resources at abundantlifestudy.com

103

3. **He is holy and righteous.** God is holy, or set apart. He is God and completely unique. There is no one like Him. His ways are perfect and right. *Psalm 7:17, 30:4, 71:14-19, 99:3, 119:7, 164*

4. **He is your Savior, Creator, Redeemer, and the Great I AM.** God is everything to you. *Exodus 3:14; Psalm 28:7-9, 71:6-8; Isaiah 43:10-13, 45:21-22; Luke 24:52-53; 1 Peter 2:9-10 (Exodus 15:2; Deuteronomy 10:21-22; Nehemiah 9:5-17; Luke 2:13-14, 20)*

5. **He is love.** God is love. It is His essence. *1 John 4:7-11 (John 3:16; Romans 5:8)*

6. **He is merciful.** You need to praise God for mercy. We all need abundant mercy, and the Lord gives it! Mercy is not getting what you deserve; it is God's desire to rescue you with compassion from trouble. (Some translations use the words love, lovingkindness, or compassion.) *Psalm 118:1-4; Micah 7:18; Titus 3:4-5; 1 Peter 1:3 (2 Chronicles 5:13, 20:21; Psalm 36:5, 63:3-5, 86:15)*

QUESTIONS TO PONDER:

1. Read *Psalm 63* and then focus on *verses 3-5*. What is a benefit of praising God? How can this help you in your Christian life and relationships? Why is it healthy to be thankful and express it?

2. What are different ways that you can praise God? In what different situations can you praise God?

3. List 10 things from Part I that you should praise God for every day. How big is this list?

4. Contemplate your praise of God. How often do you praise Him? In what ways do you praise Him? Could this use some improvement? Do you feel a greater desire to praise Him after meditating on Part I of this study?

See videos & more under resources at abundantlifestudy.com

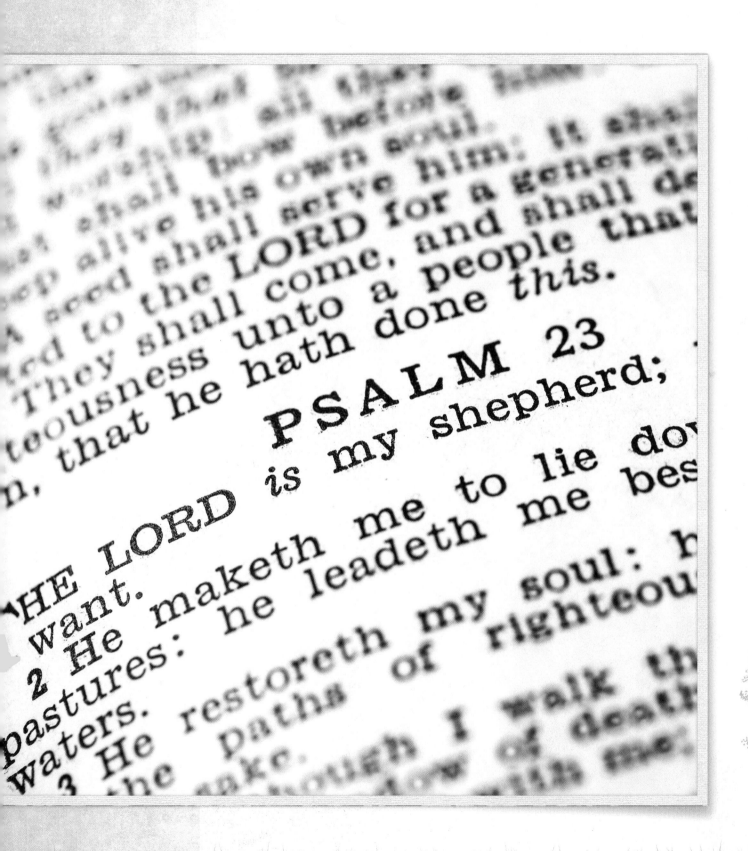

ABUNDANT WORDS
The Communication of Relationship

—≪≪≪

If you abide in Me, and My words abide in you,
you will ask what you desire, and it shall be done
for you. By this My Father is glorified, that you
bear much fruit; so you will be My disciples.
John 15:7-8 NKJV

How do we get to know someone and have a relationship with him or her? By spending time together and talking to each other. There are many ways to communicate, but verbal communication is the most meaningful and specific. Verbal communication is a word exchange. God's words to us are found in the Bible. It is the Word of God (His words to us). Prayer is talking to God and provides our words to God. The basics of a relationship with God are reading His words (Bible) and communicating with Him in prayer.

The more we talk and communicate, the more our relationship will grow. His words speak to our hearts. Reading and praying are essential. If we want to know the God who created us, who has a personal plan for our lives, and loves us enough to die for us, then we must be reading the Word of God and talking to Him. We can also communicate with God by silently sitting in His presence and listening to Him speak to our hearts. This is not burdensome because we should have an abundant desire from His abundant revelation, as studied in Part I.

See videos & more
under resources at
abundantlifestudy.com

1. **The Words of God.** In the Bible, God has revealed who He is, what He is like, and what He has done and will do. The Bible is the Word of God. It is His words to you. It is the main way He communicates to you. Jesus Christ is the living, incarnate Word of God. If you want to know Christ, you must be in His Word. A relationship has a two-way word exchange, and God has given you 66 books of His words. That is more than enough for the rest of your life! *2 Timothy 3:16-17; John 1:1-5, 14, 8:31-32, 15:7-8 (Revelation 19:11-16)*

   Eating the Word. The Bible is your spiritual food. It feeds your spirit and soul so that you can grow spiritually. Reading is eating. Newborn babies are hungry and need to eat or they will suffer from starvation. You should be hungry and eating a daily healthy diet of the Word of God. You should hunger to know God, hear what He has to say, and discover more of what He is like.

   If you do not read His Word, then you do not care to know Him or hear from Him. This is a prevalent problem today among Christians. People are reading almost everything but the Word of God. If you live the abundant life, however, it will solve this problem. You have found the cure! Because you learned in Part I how awesome God is and how much He loves you and wants to guide your life, you cannot wait to know Him and hear what He has to say to you. You should view the Bible as God's love letter to His children. *Job 23:12; 1 Peter 2:2-3; Matthew 4:4; John 6:34-35; 1 Corinthians 3:1-4; Hebrews 5:12-14 (Ezekiel 3:1-3; Revelation 10:10)*

   Hearing the Word (Listening). We spiritually "hear" with our hearts. Your heart must be right for you to hear the words of God when you read the Bible. A hardened or disinterested heart can read the Bible and hear nothing at all. It is like putting food in your mouth but then spitting it right back out. It never gets a chance to provide its nutrition. Because you are so enamored with God based upon what He has done for you, you are attentively listening when you read His Word. You should be trying to learn and hear what He has to say to you through His Word. If your heart is eager, expectant, humble, and grateful, then you will "hear." *Jeremiah 19:15; Matthew 11:15, 13:13-17; Luke 8:4-15; John 8:47, 10:27; Romans 10:17*

Meditating on the Word. You should meditate on the words of God because they are so powerful and nutritious for your heart and soul. Meditation on the Scriptures is like completely digesting your food so that you absorb it all. *Psalm 1; Joshua 1:8-9; Psalm 119:15, 23, 48, 97-99, 148; Philippians 4:8-9*

Believing/Doing the Word. Believing the Word involves doing it! Eating, hearing, and meditating on the words of God are not enough! You must also be a doer of the Word. You should obey what God says and do what He says because your heart is surrendered to His love. You need to change, and this starts with doing what God says. This is loving God. You must allow the Word to do "surgery" in your heart. *James 1:22-25; Matthew 7:24-27, 12:50; Luke 11:28; John 14:21-24; Romans 2:13; 1 John 2:3-6; Hebrews 4:12 (James 4:17; Revelation 22:7)*

Delighting in the Word. The Word of God is delightful! You should delight yourself in it because you love the Lord, who is the Word of God. *Psalm 119:16, 24, 47, 70, 77; Romans 7:22.*

2. **The Words of Prayer.** Talking to God is prayer. You can pray for God's will, help in trials, guidance, strength, mercy, forgiveness, healing, wisdom, thanksgiving, protection, and almost anything else in life. This is your part of the relationship. You need to realize that God has given you abundant access to Him! You can talk to the Creator of the universe, who is your Father and who is love, anytime you want. He wants to hear from you just like parents do from their children.

    You were created for a relationship with Him. You should be so overwhelmed by His grace, love, mercy, and provision—as you will recall from Part I—that you cannot wait to talk to Him. We could do an entire study on prayer, because it is so important. Pray! Talk to God! Praise Him. Depend upon Him. Tell Him your troubles and needs. Surrender your heart and life in words of devotion. Think about His Majestic ability to hear one person out of billions! Do not treat this as an obligation but, rather, the most amazing opportunity ever.

See videos & more under resources at abundantlifestudy.com

Jeremiah 29:11-13; 1 Samuel 2:1-10; Psalm 5:1-3; Matthew 6:5-13; Mark 1:35, 6:46; Luke 6:12-16; 1 Timothy 2:8; 1 Thessalonians 5:16-17 (Psalm 32:6; Daniel 9:4-19; Mark 14:38; Luke 1:46-55; James 5:16-18)

3. **The Words of Praise.** Praise was the subject of Lesson 13. Often expressed in words, praise is an internal state of the heart in response to God's love, salvation, grace, and mercy. Because of what God has done for you, you should abundantly praise God with abundant words of thanksgiving. *Psalm 150 (Psalm 146:1-2, 147:1, 148)*

QUESTIONS TO PONDER:

1. One of the early signs of pride is a lack of prayer. What is pride? Discuss why a lack of prayer is a sign of pride.

2. Read *Mark 1:35, 6:46,* and *Luke 6:12.* Jesus is God, yet what did He do? What does this tell you about your need for prayer? How can you make time? Did Jesus let His busy schedule stop Him from doing anything? Is being too busy an excuse? If you find that a week has gone by and you have barely prayed, is something wrong? Discuss how having a zeal and desire to know God, from what you learned in Part I of this study, is the cure for a lack of prayer.

3. Discuss eating as an analogy for reading the Word of God (Bible). Why do you eat? Why is it important to eat? What has to happen when food is put in front of you for it to help your body? It is a fact that starving people eventually lose their appetite. How might this be relevant to you today in terms of reading your Bible?

4. Read *James 1: 22-25*. Discuss the analogy God gives for only hearing His Word and not doing it.

See videos & more under resources at abundantlifestudy.com

REFLECTIONS
Week 5

Spend some time in prayer reflecting on this week's lessons. Ask God to speak to your heart and reveal to you what's important. Then spend some time answering the questions below. Write down your responses to discuss them in your small groups or as a journal entry to remember what you have learned.

INSIGHTS:

What are some of the key insights you have learned from this week's lessons? What has stood out to you? What has spoken to your heart?

Lesson 12 • Abundant Surrender

Lesson 13 • Abundant Praise

Lesson 14 • Abundant Words

APPLICATIONS:

How should you respond to what you have learned in this week's lessons? What do you need to do differently? What changes do you feel the Lord leading you to make? What specific steps can you take?

See videos & more under resources at abundantlifestudy.com

ABUNDANT GOD
The Interaction of Relationship

$\ll\ll\ll$

And this is eternal life, that they may know You, the only true God, and Jesus Christ whom You have sent.

John 17:3 NKJV

When we respond to God's abundant revelation with abundant surrender, praise, worship, gratitude, prayer and reading His word to seek a relationship with Him, God responds back! When His children run to Him in gratitude to know Him, obey Him, and depend upon Him, He is delighted and abundantly responds to us. We were created for a relationship with the God who made us and died for us so we can finally know Him. The cross is Jesus' declaration that He will do anything to save us so we can know Him and have an eternal relationship with Him. He is the initiator in the entire process. We respond to God, and then He abundantly responds to us. He is waiting for us to respond so He can respond back!

VERSES TO READ, STUDY, AND MEDITATE ON:

1. **God's Answers.** God answers prayer. Sometimes it is no, and often His answers are delayed, but He does answer. He answers prayer in many ways. You must pay attention to what is going on around you, because sometimes you find God's answers through your circumstances. At other times He answers through His Word using particular Scriptures. He can also speak to your heart and guide you by using His peace or disruption of that peace to show you His will. We cannot review

See videos & more under resources at abundantlifestudy.com

answered prayer in detail in this study, but we can know that God does answer according to His will, in His timing, and in His way! *2 Samuel 5:19; 2 Kings 19:15-20; Daniel 10:12; Matthew 7:7-12; John 14:12-14; Ephesians 3:20; James 4:1-5; 1 John 5:14-15 (Genesis 20:17; 1 Samuel 8:6-7, 23:2-4, 30:8; Jeremiah 33:3; Matthew 21:21-22; John 16:23-24)*

2. **God's Presence.** When you draw near to God, He draws near to you. This is an awareness of His presence that He makes spiritually known to you. Remember, He is not far, but lives inside of you and is all around you! He can use this to strengthen and encourage you in times of need or to simply bless your soul for seeking Him. *Psalm 16:11, 46:10, 63:1-11, 145:18; Isaiah 57:15; John 14:19-23; Romans 8:16; James 4:7-8 (Psalm 21:6, 95:2; 1 Corinthians 10:16-17)*

3. **God's Filling.** Filling is a misnomer that can give you the wrong understanding. God is all around you and lives within you. You already possess God's living presence. When you draw close to God and seek His presence, will, and a relationship with Him, He responds by manifesting Himself to you through His peace, joy, and control of your heart. You are spiritually content and filled with peace from His presence. *Isaiah 58:11; Matthew 5:6; John 6:26-27, 35; Colossians 1:9; Ephesians 3:14-19*

   Filled with Love, Joy, Peace, and Hope. When you are in a right relationship with the Lord, He fills your heart with His love, joy, and peace so that you may abound in hope. His peace guards your heart and mind and strengthens you. *Isaiah 26:3-4; John 14:27, 15:11; Acts 2:28; Romans 5:5, 15:13; Philippians 4:6-7*

   Filled with the Holy Spirit. This means to be controlled by the Holy Spirit. You have the Holy Spirit, who is God, living inside you! In the Bible there seems to be two kinds of Spirit filling. In one type, God sovereignly empowers a person to accomplish His will in a specific situation. It is not in response to prayer or based upon performance. We will not study this because it is not in our control. If God wants to empower you for His service, then He will. You do not need to focus on empowerment but on surrender and obedience to His will. He will take care of the rest. In the other type of filling you do have a role, and it is critical!

When you surrender to God and seek to serve Him with your heart, then you allow the power of God in you to take control and guide your life. You unleash the guiding and influencing power of the Holy Spirit. It is supposed to be a continual state of fullness and not a specific one-time event. You are to be filled and keep on being filled by allowing God to have His way with you. This is why surrender and devotion from gratitude and love are so important. You need all of the power that is available to you to live in this fallen world in your fallen body. This issue will be discussed in Part III, because even when we are trying our best and are "filled" we will still struggle and fail. You need God living within you, controlling your heart, thoughts, motives, words, and actions.

It is important to understand that this is a process related to spiritual growth, which we will study later in Part III. Over time, as you stay surrendered and let God guide and control your life for His purpose, you will slowly yield more and more to His will. It takes time for God to work on you so that you surrender increasingly more areas of your life. Spiritual growth involves God having increasing control over your heart and life (i.e., more filled).

It is important not to focus on being filled or experiencing being filled. You should not be preoccupied with this. There is no single moment or magic experience that provides instant victory in the Christian life. You need to focus on loving, surrendering, and seeking the will of God for your life. If you do this, then God will provide whatever power or blessings of His Spirit that you need. If you are surrendered and focused on God with your whole heart, then you will be controlled by the Holy Spirit (i.e., filled). If you have the abundant response you have been studying, then you will be abundantly filled. It is not about you and your state of spirituality, but God and His will and purpose for your life that brings Him glory. Focus on Him! *Ephesians 5:17-18; Luke 4:1; Acts 6:3, 5, 7:55, 11:24, 13:52*

See videos & more under resources at abundantlifestudy.com

4. **God's Guidance.** The Lord provides His guidance when you are submitting in gratitude to His plan for your life and seeking His will. When you open your heart to God's plan, then He establishes it for you. Your desires will be the Lord's because He has put them on your heart.

   Our Thoughts:
   Proverbs 16:3; Jeremiah 31:33; John 14:26

   Our Hearts:
   Ezra 1:5, 7:27; Nehemiah 2:12, 7:5; Psalm 37:4-5, 119:36;
   Proverbs 21:1; John 16:13

   Our Steps:
   Psalm 37:23, 40:2, 119:133; Proverbs 3:5-7, 20:24;
   Isaiah 58:11; Philippians 2:13 (Psalm 31:3, 32:8, 73:24)

   His Prayers:
   John 17:20-24; Romans 8:27, 34; Hebrews 7:25; 1 John 2:1

   His Wisdom:
   Proverbs 2:1-22; Ephesians 1:17-20; James 1:5-8, 3:17
   (1 Corinthians 1:24)

   His Anointing: See Lesson 7 in Part I to review this concept.
   1 John 2:20-27

5. **God's Strength.** God has made His power available to you when you call on Him and desire to walk in His will. He can strengthen you for service and to endure trials. *1 Samuel 30:6; Nehemiah 8:10; Psalm 28:7-9, 46:1; Isaiah 40:31, 20:6; Acts 1:8; 2 Corinthians 12:9; Ephesians 3:16, 6:10; 2 Timothy 4:17 (Psalm 18, 27:1; Colossians 1:9-11; Hebrews 2:18; 1 Peter 1:5)*

1. Discuss how God answers prayer. Use some of the verses given in this lesson as starting points.

2. Discuss how God puts things on your heart. How can you test them to see if they are truly from God?

3. Read *Ephesians 5:17-21*. The Greek here literally means "keep on being filled," a continual state of being filled, not a one-time event. If Paul commanded it, then what does this imply? Discuss Paul's contrast between being filled with the Spirit and being drunk with alcohol. In *verses 19-21*, what are the results of being filled? Why might the Holy Spirit desire these things for your life?

See videos & more under resources at abundantlifestudy.com

ABUNDANT REPENTANCE
The Conviction of Relationship

─≪≪≪≪

I acknowledged my sin to You, and my iniquity I have
not hidden. I said, "I will confess my transgressions to
the Lord," and You forgave the iniquity of my sin.
Psalm 32:5 NKJV

Conviction is an inner pronouncement and convincing of the soul that it is guilty before God. It is a bringing to light and exposure of sin in a way that is known and shown to be true. Conviction is often felt and experienced as guilt, shame, fear, and a strong, uncomfortable inner sense of wrongdoing before God. Anger can also be a sign of conviction, as a result of fear or the frustration of being convicted. The conviction is focused on personal change leading to holiness and becoming more like Jesus Christ. It is not a conviction of condemnation, but of love from the Creator who cares about His children and knows the destructive power of sin. Conviction is a ministry of the Holy Spirit that is designed to bring us to repentance.

Repentance is a turning away from sin and towards God. Our grief and sorrow are directed towards God because we have sinned against Him. There is a deep and strong sense of grief that motivates us to change because we have sinned against our heavenly Father. This includes an acknowledgement that we are a sinner before God, which comes from a heart that is trusting in the blood of Jesus Christ to cover our sins. It is part of the ongoing state of "believing" in Jesus by trusting His work on the cross to cover our sins. It is the Holy Spirit within a person that enables him or her to be conscious, grieved, and repentant over sin. He creates a sense of guilt and a need to be restored to the Father. It is

See videos & more
under resources at
abundantlifestudy.com

the next natural step after conviction of sin. Yes, in fact, many refer to this type of repentant grief as "Godly sorrow."

The closer we get to Jesus Christ by continued surrender, prayer, worship, and reading His Word, the more we realize how sinful we are. The more time we spend studying the Word of God, the more we will be aware of our sin. This is actually a sign of spiritual growth and health. It creates a healthy heart that recognizes the need for grace and is grateful for the blessings of God's salvation. We love God more and more because we begin to realize just how much He has done for us by dying for all of our sins.

This love and gratitude for Christ creates a heart that does not want to sin against Him. When we do, we are grieved and we repent. Because our hearts are filled with gratitude, reverence, and a desire to know God, we immediately want to restore our relationship with Him. Repentance keeps us humble and dependent, and it keeps our relationship with Him healthy. Our relationship with the Lord should be characterized by abundant repentance, because we will continue to sin and make mistakes. It is a sign that we are aware and care. The goal will be for us to sin less and less, but we will never be sinless.

VERSES TO READ, STUDY, AND MEDITATE ON:

1. **Awareness of Sin in God's Presence.** God is perfectly holy and sinless. The closer you get to Him, the more aware you are of your sinfulness. This should make you revere and love Him more for who He is and for the grace and mercy given to you in Christ. *Job 42:1-6; Isaiah 6:1-8; Luke 5:1-8*

2. **Conviction of Sin from the Word of God.** *Nehemiah 8:1-9:3; Acts 2:36-38, 7:48-54; 2 Timothy 3:16-17; Hebrews 4:12*

3. **Conviction by the Holy Spirit.** *John 16:7-11; Psalm 38*

4. **Grieving the Holy Spirit.** The Holy Spirit, who is God, is also a person. Because He is perfectly righteous, holy, and sinless, any sin that enters your life causes Him to grieve. Sin causes Him to be sorrowful and have grief over your sin that can sometimes be internally sensed and felt because He lives within you. This grief is experienced completely

differently than feeling sorry for or convicted about your sin. It is an inner sense of grief and sorrow that you realize is coming from God within you. This working of the Holy Spirit within you should cause you to repent. Note: Grieving the Holy Spirit hinders His divine power to work in you, as well. *Ephesians 4:25-32; Isaiah 63:10*

5. **Repentance to God.** *2 Chronicles 7:14; Psalm 32, 51; Ezekiel 14:6-8, 18:30-32; Romans 2:4; 2 Corinthians 7:10; 1 John 1:8-10; Revelation 2:1-5*

QUESTIONS TO PONDER:

1. Read *Psalm 32*. The context of this psalm and of *Psalm 51* is that they were written after David had committed adultery with Bathsheba and had her husband killed to cover it up. He was trying to hide and cover up his sin. David had delayed repentance even under conviction (see *2 Samuel chapters 11 and 12*).

    List all of the internal feelings David was having from his sin, as described in *verses 3 and 4*.

    In *verse 3* David says, "When I kept silent..." What was he silent about? To whom was he silent? What had he failed to do? To whom was he acknowledging this?

See videos & more under resources at abundantlifestudy.com

2. Read *Psalm 51*. Whom did David think he had sinned against? Why?

   In this psalm, for what is David crying out to God? Is it simply mercy and forgiveness? What else is he asking for? Why?

   In *verses 11, 12, 14*, and *17* David describes the effects of his sin. What are they?

   What happened to David as he delayed his repentance?

3. Read *Ephesians 4:25-32*, focusing on *verse 30*. What is the context for this verse, as discussed in *verses 25-29*? Read *Isaiah 63:10*. What caused the Holy Spirit to be grieved?

4. Read *2 Corinthians 7:10*. What is the difference between worldly sorrow and Godly sorrow? What is the difference between genuine repentance and feeling guilty, sorry, or remorseful?

See videos & more under resources at abundantlifestudy.com

ABUNDANT LOVE FOR GOD
The Heart of Relationship

≪≪≪≪

You shall love the Lord your God with all your heart,
with all your soul, and with all your mind.

Matthew 22:37 NKJV

The word for love, as used in the New Testament to talk about loving God, is agape. Agape love is giving that is unselfish, unconditional, self-sacrificing, and centered on others not ourselves. Agape love is not something that we have naturally. It comes from God because He is agape love. God pours His love into our hearts by the power of the Holy Spirit so that we can love Him and others. His love flows through us to others. Agape love for God is unselfish, unconditional, God-centered obedience to His will and Word while giving oneself to Him from a grateful and reverent heart. The Great Commandment is to agape love God with all our heart, soul, and mind—or our whole person and existence. The heart of love is surrender and obedience. Because God has so loved us, we should love Him and others. (Loving others will be discussed in Part III.) This type of love is our final and ultimate response to God and is the culmination of everything we have studied so far.

VERSES TO READ, STUDY, AND MEDITATE ON:

1. **God is love.** *1 John 4:7-8, 16*

2. **God loves you.** God proved His love on the cross. *Jeremiah 31:3; John 3:16; Romans 5:8; 1 John 4:9-11, 16*

See videos & more
under resources at
abundantlifestudy.com

3. **God gives you His love.** He is the only source of the agape love that you need. *Romans 5:5; Ephesians 3:19; 2 Timothy 1:7; 1 John 4:12-13 (2 Thessalonians 3:5)*

4. **Love is your response to His love.** He loved you first. You should abundantly respond to His love with love for Him. He died for you. You should live to obey Him. (Love for others will be discussed in Part III.) *1 John 4:19 (Psalm 18:1-3, 116:1-4; 2 Corinthians 5:14-15; Ephesians 5:2)*

5. **Love is the Great Commandment.** *Deuteronomy 6:5-6; Matthew 22:35-39 (Deuteronomy 10:12, 11:1, 11:13, chapter 30)*

6. **Love is obedience to the Word of God.** Jesus defined loving Him as obeying His Word. His Word is the Word of God (Bible). *John 14:21-24; 1 John 5:3*

7. **Love is walking in faith.** Biblical faith is God speaks-you hear-you obey. Obeying the Word of God is loving God. Biblical faith expresses itself in love. *Genesis 22:1-19; Galatians 5:6; Hebrews 11:1-9*

8. **Loving God is a test of salvation.** Jesus clarified that those who are genuinely saved do the will of God. They obey His words, His commands, and His personal will for their lives out of love, not obligation. *Matthew 7:21-23; 1 John 2:3-5, 4:7-8*

9. **Love is surrender and worship.** Jesus Christ on the cross is the ultimate example of love. He surrendered His life so that you could have life. Because Jesus gave all of Himself for you, you should give yourself back to Him. Surrender and worship are expressions of love that Jesus exemplified. *John 15:13; Romans 5:8; Ephesians 5:2 (Leviticus 1:1-9)*

10. **Love is exclusive.** You must get rid of anything that comes in the way of your relationship with Him. *Exodus 20:3-4; Joshua 24:19-20; Matthew 4:10, 6:24; James 4:4; 1 John 2:15-17*

11. **Love takes precedence and priority.** Jesus should be number one in your life. You should love Him so much that even your love for your family is nothing compared to your love for God. *Luke 14:26; Acts 20:24; Revelation 12:11*

12. **Love is everything.** Without agape love you are nothing. *1 Corinthians 13*

13. **Love fulfills the Law.** On the cross Jesus loved the Father by obeying Him. He also loved you by dying in your place. The cross is formed by Jesus loving God vertically and Jesus loving you horizontally. On the cross Jesus fulfilled the two Great Commandments: to love God and to love others. When you love God you do not have any other gods or idols or use His name in vain. You also obey like Jesus did. *Matthew 22:35-40; Romans 13:8-10; Galatians 5:14*

QUESTIONS TO PONDER:

1. Read *Deuteronomy 6:5-6, Matthew 22:35-38*, and *John 14:21-24*. What is the Great Commandment? How does Jesus define loving Him? What implications does this have for your need to study the Bible? How can you obey if you do not know what God says? How can you obey the Great Commandment without reading and knowing the Word of God?

2. Read *John 14:21-24*. What did Jesus promise for those who love Him? What does this mean? Discuss how this is an incredible incentive to read the Word of God and keep it (i.e., do it).

See videos & more under resources at abundantlifestudy.com

3. Read *Matthew 22:35-40*, *Romans 13:8-10*, *Galatians 5:14*, and *James 2:8-11*.

Draw a vertical line to make the vertical part of a cross. Label it "Loving God." Draw a horizontal line to complete the cross. Label it "Loving Others." What supports the cross bar of loving others? Discuss how this demonstrates that loving God is primary.

Jesus said, "All the law and the prophets 'hang' on these two commandments." Who "hung" on these two commandments?

4. Read *Genesis 22:1-19* and *Hebrews 11:1-9*. Since love is obedience to the Word of God, how did Abraham demonstrate his love for God? What critical moment in history did Abraham and Isaac foreshadow? Bonus: Where is Mount Moriah compared to where Jesus was crucified? See *2 Chronicles 3:1*.

See videos & more under resources at abundantlifestudy.com

ABUNDANT HEALTH
The Wellness of Relationship

→←←←←

Do not be wise in your own eyes; fear the Lord and shun evil. This will bring health to your body and nourishment to your bones.

Proverbs 3:7-8 NIV

You cannot grow unless you are healthy. This is true physically and spiritually. Spiritual health is essential for spiritual growth. What is a state of spiritual health? What is a spiritually healthy heart that is beating strong for God? It is a combination of everything that we have studied! Holiness is spiritual health to our spirit as physical health is to our physical bodies. The "germs" of sin can cause our hearts to be sick and diseased. A spiritually healthy Christian has a heart filled with the knowledge of the things we studied in Part I.

From Bible study and meditation the person understands God's abundant grace and all of the amazing things that God has done for him or her, which reveals His person and love. The person's heart is surrendered from gratitude, awe, and wonder. From the love for God, the heart is filled with praise, the words of God from Scripture, and repentance (when needed). It is controlled (filled) by the Holy Spirit. There is an interactive, abundant relationship which is abundantly healthy! A healthy heart will produce abundant results, as we will discover in Part III of this study. The abundant results lead to increasing holiness. Holiness is spiritual health because we become more and more like Jesus with less and less sin in our lives.

See videos & more under resources at abundantlifestudy.com

It is important for us to understand that abundant results are the natural outflow of a healthy, abundant relationship with the Lord Jesus Christ. If we are lacking in results, then we can trace it back to an unhealthy heart that is not in a right relationship with the Lord. Recall that the impetus and fuel that sparked and will maintain our relationship with God was surrender because of who He is, what He is like, and what He has done for us. In this respect, a lack of results from poor spiritual health can be traced back to a lack of knowledge and Biblical illiteracy. Poor spiritual health comes from more than simply not reading our Bibles, however. We must allow the Word to change us. We must submit ourselves to the Word and do what it says.

VERSES TO READ, STUDY, AND MEDITATE ON:

1. **Fed.** A healthy heart is well fed by a steady diet of the Word of God. The Word of God is your spiritual food. Spiritual health requires spiritual nourishment. *Matthew 4:4; 1 Peter 2:2-3; Hebrews 5:12-14 (John 6:35; 1 Corinthians 3:1-4; Job 23:12; Ezekiel 3:3)*

2. **Filled.** A healthy heart is filled with and pumps out praise, love, joy, peace, and hope. The heart must be filled to have proper function and output. It is filled with the things of God and eternity. An empty heart, or a heart filled with the wrong things, will have heart failure. *Psalm 9:1-2, 96:4-9; Matthew 5:6; Romans 5:5, 15:13; John 6:26-27, 35; Ephesians 3:14-19; Philippians 4:6-9; Colossians 1:9, 3:15-16*

3. **Controlled.** A healthy heart has a proper pace and rhythm that are controlled by the Holy Spirit. This comes from a state of surrender and giving your heart to God. The New Testament calls this being "filled" with the Holy Spirit. (Recall our study from Lesson 15.) *Ephesians 5:18 (Luke 4:1; Acts 6:3, 5, 7:55, 11:24, 13:52)*

4. **Exercised.** A healthy heart requires exercise and training to have endurance and strength. This comes from a relationship with Jesus Christ in which He works on our hearts through His Word, prayer, worship, and seeing us through life's struggles and tribulations. An exercised heart is active for the Lord. *Acts 20:24; 1 Corinthians 9:24-27; Philippians 3:13-14; 2 Timothy 2:5, 4:7; Hebrews 12:1-2 (1 Peter 1:6-9; 2 Peter 1:1-10)*

5. **Listening and Hearing.** A healthy heart must be soft and pliable, not hardened. A soft heart is able to hear and listen to the Word of God. It is listening, eager, and willing to obey from gratitude, trust, and reverence. A hardened heart will not receive the Word of God. It is spiritually deaf and blind. Its soil is not penetrable. *Proverbs 28:14; Matthew 13:3-23; Mark 16:14; John 10:27, 12:37-41 (Exodus 8:15, 32; Ephesians 4:17-19)*

6. **Clean.** A healthy heart is "clean" and fertile. It is not polluted with idols and the cares and riches of this world which hinder the Word of God from changing it. It has no "weeds" or "rocks." *Mark 4:10-20; 1 John 2:15-17 (Luke 8:9-15)*

7. **Humble.** A healthy heart is humble and not prideful. It is dependent upon the Lord for its desires, thoughts, and motives because it knows it is desperately wicked without Him. A humble heart is needy and teachable. Jesus Christ humbled Himself and so should you. *Numbers 12:3; 2 Chronicles 7:14; 2 Kings 22:19; Proverbs 3:7-8, 11:2, 16:19, 29:23; Psalm 25:9, 51:17, 147:6; Isaiah 66:2; Micah 6:8; Philippians 2:8; James 4:10; 1 Peter 5:5-7 (Isaiah 57:15; Daniel 10:12)*

8. **Connected.** Spiritual health also comes from being an active member of a local church. God gave us the local church as a place for believers to serve, grow, fellowship, and mature in their faith. *Acts 2:40-47, 20:7; Ephesians 2:19; 1 Peter 3:8; Romans 14:19; Hebrews 10:24-25; 1 Corinthians 11:17-22; 1 Timothy 3:15*

QUESTIONS TO PONDER:

1. Read *Matthew 13:3-9, 13:18-23; Mark 4:10-20;* and *Luke 8:4-15.* Consider the four types of hearts in this parable. What distinguished the good heart from the other three?

See videos & more under resources at abundantlifestudy.com

What were the problems with each of the other three? What causes these problems?

What happens to the Word of God in each of them?

Why was the Word being sown? Why does Jesus talk about the Word of God and the heart?

How do you make sure you have a good and healthy heart?

If you have one of the other three types, what should you do to fix it?

2. Discuss why daily surrender and seeking the Lord's will for your life is absolutely essential to spiritual health.

3. Read *Psalm 119:11*. How is this part of a healthy heart? Why?

4. Read *Matthew 6:19-21*. What kind of treasure should you be collecting to have a healthy heart?

5. Read *John 10:1-30*. Find as many signs of health in these passages as you can. Look for signs and aspects of relationship.

See videos & more
under resources at
abundantlifestudy.com

REFLECTIONS
Week 6

Spend some time in prayer reflecting on this week's lessons. Ask God to speak to your heart and reveal to you what's important. Then spend some time answering the questions below. Write down your responses to discuss them in your small groups or as a journal entry to remember what you have learned.

INSIGHTS:

What are some of the key insights you have learned from this week's lessons? What has stood out to you? What has spoken to your heart?

Lesson 15 • Abundant God

Lesson 16 • Abundant Repentance

Lesson 17 • Abundant Love for God

Lesson 18 • Abundant Health

APPLICATIONS:

How should you respond to what you have learned in this week's lessons? What do you need to do differently? What changes do you feel the Lord leading you to make? What specific steps can you take?

See videos & more under resources at abundantlifestudy.com

PART II
The Healthy Heart

A healthy heart has an abundant relationship with Jesus Christ empowered by the abundant revelation and grace studied in Part I of this study. It is surrendered and seeking God from gratitude, awe, and wonder because it knows Who God is, what He has done, and what He is like.

The healthy Christian heart is full of praise for God and the Word of God. It is etched with God's will, filled with His love, and loves Him back by obeying His Word. Faith, hope, and love fill its chambers while repentance and prayer are its pulse. It beats from opportunity not obligation and from a passionate desire to know God not expectation. The healthy heart is strong, exercised, and filled with the Holy Spirit, which enables the entire spiritual person to be transformed into the image of Jesus Christ.

HEART EXAMINATION

Since a healthy heart is vital to Part III of this study and your spiritual growth, it's time for a quick heart examination based upon what you have studied in Parts I and II. Think positively! Look for areas you can improve and bring them to God. He loves you and wants to heal and strengthen your heart. Below are some questions to ponder to get you started. Be honest and ask God to examine your heart.

Search me, O God, and know my heart; test me and know my anxious thoughts. See if there is any offensive way in me, and lead me in the way everlasting. Psalm 139:23-24 NIV

Surrender
Are you seeking God's will and His plan for your life daily?
Are you giving yourself to Him from gratitude, love, and a desire to know Him?
Do you earnestly desire to allow Jesus to make you the person He wants you to be?
Who is on the throne of your heart? God or you?

Praise
Do you praise God for Who He is, what He is like, and what He has already done for you in Christ?
Do you have a time when you worship God and thank Him?

Communication
Is your heart being fed the Word of God on a regular basis? Are you seeking God in His Word?
Do you have a daily time of prayer and reading the Word of God?
Are you listening for Him to speak to your heart and then obeying what He says?
Is the Lord guiding your life and helping you through its struggles and challenges?

Repentance
Are you sensitive to sin in your life and repenting of it when you make a mistake?
Does your heart want to please God and avoid sin as much as possible because you love Him?

Love
Do you love God by obeying His Word? This requires that you are reading and studying His Word to know what He says (*John 14:21-24*).
Do you know that God loves you personally?
Are God and His will number one in your life?

PART III
ABUNDANT RESULTS

Transformation

WEEK 7

LESSON 19 • **ABUNDANT GROWTH:** THE NEW MAN MATURES

LESSON 20 • **ABUNDANT GODLINESS:** THE NEW MAN BLOSSOMS

WEEK 8

LESSON 21 • **ABUNDANT STRUGGLE:** THE NEW MAN STRUGGLES

LESSON 22 • **ABUNDANT SUFFERING:** THE NEW MAN SUFFERS

LESSON 23 • **ABUNDANT VICTORY:** THE NEW MAN SUCCEEDS

Fruit

WEEK 9

LESSON 24 • **ABUNDANT LOVE FOR OTHERS:** THE FOCUS OF LOVE

LESSON 25 • **ABUNDANT GIVING:** THE GIVING OF LOVE

WEEK 10

LESSON 26 • **ABUNDANT SERVICE:** THE SERVANT OF LOVE

LESSON 27 • **ABUNDANT HARVEST:** THE GOAL OF LOVE

See videos & more
under resources at
abundantlifestudy.com

PART III OVERVIEW

TRANSFORMATION

≪≪≪≪≪

And we, who with unveiled faces all reflect the Lord's glory, are
being transformed into his likeness with ever-increasing glory,
which comes from the Lord, who is the Spirit.

2 Corinthians 3:18 NIV

An abundant response to God causes an abundantly healthy relationship with Him. This results in spiritual transformation and fruit. We are gradually transformed by the power of the Holy Spirit as we continue one day at a time to surrender to God from gratitude, awe, and wonder as we walk in His will and plan for our lives. In continuing to seek Him in prayer, in worship and in the Word of God (Bible), we will begin to grow spiritually and be transformed into the image of Jesus Christ. We will become more and more like the Lord!

This process is called sanctification. It is slow and gradual, and it is never fully completed while we are alive here on earth. It requires hard work and personal discipline, but because our motivation is from love and gratitude for the incredible grace God has given us (see Part I: Abundant Revelation), this should not be a burden. The transformation process is not without its struggles, failures, and challenges. Spiritual growth requires trials and difficulties, it tests our faith, and it even requires failures from which we can learn. Yes, the abundant life is not all fun and pleasure. Despite these struggles, there is still abundant joy, comfort, and victory promised by God!

FRUIT

Abide in Me, and I in you. As the branch cannot bear fruit of itself, unless it abides in the vine, neither can you, unless you abide in Me. I am the vine, you are the branches. He who abides in Me, and I in him, bears much fruit; for without Me you can do nothing.

John 15:4-5 NKJV

As you are being transformed by God you will begin to produce "fruit" that glorifies God. Spiritual fruit in its essence is agape love. This can be simply defined as unselfish giving of yourself to others and to God. These are the two Great Commandments: to love God with all your heart and to love others as yourself. The fulfillment of these commandments will be natural and will flow from the relationship and state of spiritual health that you have studied. This fruit of love will have many effects on others around you as you serve them, love them, teach them, and reach them with the Gospel of Jesus Christ. Because you are surrendered and seeking God's will and are filled (controlled) by the Holy Spirit, you will be servants living for the Lord and His will, glory, and coming kingdom. You will be giving yourself to others and to the Lord. You will impact others for eternity by God working through you! You will be abundantly satisfied from nothing else.

See videos & more under resources at abundantlifestudy.com

- TRANSFORMATION -
ABUNDANT GROWTH
The New Man Matures

—≪≪≪≪—

As newborn babes, desire the pure milk of the word
that you may grow thereby, if indeed you have tasted
that the Lord is gracious.
1 Peter 2:2-3 NKJV

We have already studied how the Word of God is our spiritual food (Lesson 14) and how a healthy heart is well fed by a steady diet of the Word of God (Lesson 18). Spiritual growth requires spiritual health and nourishment. If the new man is created by a new birth, being "born again" (Lesson 4), then he is a spiritual baby at birth. A baby needs to grow and mature. Growth and maturity require food, health, and a proper environment that fosters both.

This concept is critical because, as we will learn in the next few lessons, it is this new man along with the power of the Holy Spirit that will battle sin, the sinful nature/flesh, the enemy, and the world. Although God provides the means for growth and the power for victory, He leaves it up to us to tap into this power by choosing to grow and mature. If a person fails to grow and remains a "baby," that person will be dominated by his or her sinful nature/flesh and have little to no victory over sin.

See videos & more
under resources at
abundantlifestudy.com

VERSES TO READ, STUDY, AND MEDITATE ON:

1. **Spiritual Growth.** Spiritual growth has many aspects. Everything that you will study about abundant transformation is part of the growth process. *Psalm 1:1-6, 92:12-15*

   Growth in Love. *1 Thessalonians 3:12; Philippians 1:9-11; Ephesians 3:14-19*

   Growth in Knowledge, Understanding, and Wisdom. You can gain a lot of knowledge from the Word of God, but unless you apply that knowledge, it profits you nothing. Understanding is seeing the personal application, whereas wisdom is actually doing it. If you grow in the knowledge of God and His grace, goodness, and love for you, then this should positively affect your practical daily relationship with Him. *Ephesians 1:15-21, 4:15; Colossians 1:9-12; 2 Peter 2:1-8, 3:18*

   Growth in Faith. Faith is something of which you can never have enough. You need to grow in faith, and this comes from reading and applying the Word of God. As you "eat, digest, and assimilate" the Word of God into you, you grow in faith. Faith is a certainty of God in the heart that comes from hearing the Word of God and results in obeying the Word of God, which is love. Faith expresses itself in love. Another Biblical definition of faith is: God speaks—you hear—you obey. *Romans 10:17; 2 Corinthians 10:15; 2 Thessalonians 1:3-4; 1 Peter 1:6-9; Jude 20-21 (Psalm 27; Luke 17:5-10; Acts 6:5)*

   Growth in Relationship. As you mature and grow in the Lord, your relationship with Him will grow and become more real to you. A child can interact with his father better than a baby can and will have a better understanding of who his dad is and what he does for him. An adult, on the other hand, is even more mature and has spent more time with his father and thus will have a much deeper understanding of him. Time spent together, memories, and going through life together build and grow a relationship. The same is true of your relationship with God. *John 8:31-32, 15:1-16, 17:3; 1 John 2:24-25*

Growth in Dependency and Need. Christian maturity brings increasing dependency on God for everything. As you grow and get closer to the Lord, you become more and more aware at deeper and deeper levels of how sinful you are. The more you understand the truth from the Word of God, the more you realize you really know nothing at all. You begin to realize that you need the Lord in every thought, motive, word, deed, and circumstance of your life. This creates humility, dependency, and amazing gratefulness leading to surrender because of what Jesus has done by rescuing you from sin. *Psalm 27, 73:25-28; Isaiah 55:8-9; Mark 2:17; John 15:5; Romans 7:18 (read 7:13-25), 8:26; Philippians 4:10-13 (Psalm 103, 119)*

2. **Renewing the Mind.** The new man, born as a spiritual baby, will also have to renew his mind. Although he is born with a new mind and now has the Holy Spirit, there is still a lot of work to be done. Many things need to be learned and unlearned. This is part of "growing up." The mind and heart are integrally related in ways that we do not understand, but the need for growth and change is necessary and clear in Scripture. You need your mind to be surrendered, unified with God and others, selfless (a servant at heart), heavenly/eternally focused, peaceful, and content. These are the hallmark qualities of a healthy, mature mind of a growing Christian.

   Surrendered Mind. As you have studied, surrender is the key. There is no transformation without surrender. Your growth will be stunted to the degree that you do not give all of yourself to God and His plan for your life. *Luke 22:42; John 4:34; Romans 12:1-2; Philippians 1:1*

   Renewed Mind. Your mind will be renewed. The way you think will change. *Romans 12:1-2; Ephesians 4:23-24; Philippians 3:7-8; Hebrews 9:14*

   Meditating Mind. Your mind should be meditating on the Word of God. Jesus is the Word of God. The Word is your food and power for change. *Joshua 1:8; Philippians 4:8 (Psalm 1; John 1:1-3, 8:31-32)*

   Sober/Sensible/Controlled Mind. Your mind will be clear, sensible, and controlled by the Holy Spirit. *Titus 2:6; Romans 12:3; 1 Peter 1:13, 4:7, 5:8; 2 Timothy 1:7*

See videos & more under resources at abundantlifestudy.com

Unified Mind. Your mind will be unified with the Lord's will and with your brothers and sisters in the body of Christ. *Romans 15:5-6; 1 Corinthians 1:10; 2 Corinthians 13:11; Philippians 2:1-2, 3:15-16; Hebrews 8:10 (Romans 12:16; 1 Peter 3:8)*

Servant/Selfless Mind of Christ. The heart of Christianity is serving others with the love of Jesus Christ. As you become more like Jesus, you will become a greater servant. *Mark 10:45; 1 Corinthians 2:16; Philippians 2:3-11*

Christ-Centered Mind. You should be focused on the Lord and His grace, love, and presence. He should be number one. You should be infatuated with Him! *Isaiah 26:3-4; Matthew 22:37; Philippians 3:8-16; 1 Peter 1:13-14 (Titus 2:11-14)*

Heavenly/Eternal Mind. You should develop an eternal paradigm of life focused on the things that will matter and last in eternity. You should see the world through Biblical glasses and be focused on the will of God and His coming kingdom. *Matthew 6:19-21; 2 Corinthians 4:16-5:11; Colossians 3:1-3; Philippians 1:19-26, 3:19-21; 2 Peter 3:10-13 (Psalm 119:36-37; Romans 2:7, 8:5-8; 2 Timothy 2:4; 1 John 2:15-17; Jude 20-21)*

Peaceful/Content/Guarded Mind. God will guard your heart with His peace when you are in a right relationship with Him and meditating on Him and His Word. This is a blessing from God and is a result of everything you studied above. *Isaiah 26:3-4; Philippians 4:6-7 (2 Corinthians 10:3-5)*

Secure/Certain Mind. You will be more and more certain of your salvation and the hope of Heaven as you grow and mature. You will know that you are going to be with the Lord forever, which brings increasing joy and hope. *Romans 8:15-16; Philippians 1:21-26; 1 John 3:18-23, 5:13 (2 Corinthians 5:1-11; Galatians 4:6-7)*

3. **Cleansing the Heart.** Your heart is the control center of your life. Even though you receive a new heart, there is still a war within you between the new man and the old sinful nature/flesh that wants to

contaminate your new heart. The growth process involves a gradual cleansing of your heart. As you abide in the Lord and His Word, He removes the dirt and contaminants that do not belong there. *Psalm 51:10; 2 Corinthians 7:1; 1 Thessalonians 4:3; 1 John 3:1-3 (John 15:1-8, 17:17-19; Ephesians 5:25-27; Titus 2:14; James 4:8)*

4. **Putting on the Armor.** Living the Christian life is war. This is another paradigm shift of the mind. The enemy is real and will be discussed in an upcoming lesson. God has made available His armor for you to use, but you must put it on. A growing Christian will be using the armor and gaining battle experience. He or she will learn how to use the different pieces of armor and be increasingly aware of the war. If you look at the different parts of the armor, you will see that many of them are related to the Word of God. You have to know what the armor is to fully utilize its benefits. *Ephesians 6:10-20; 1 Thessalonians 5:8; 2 Timothy 2:3-4; 1 Peter 5:8 (Psalm 18, 144:1-2; Romans 13:11-14; 2 Corinthians 6:7)*

QUESTIONS TO PONDER:

1. To understand the need for Christian growth, explore the analogy of being born again as a spiritual baby. What happens if a baby does not get enough food? What kinds of problems do starving people have?

   Read *1 Corinthians 3:1-4*. What was the problem with the Corinthians? What was the cause?

Read *Hebrews 5:12-14*. What problem was the writer addressing? How does spiritual starvation affect your Christian witness and your ability to be used by the Lord for His glory? Is a starving baby able to realize the problem? Does a baby know he is a baby? How might this affect a certainty of salvation?

2. Read *Philippians 2:1-11*. What kind of mind should you have? Describe the mind of Jesus Christ. What qualities should you be striving for?

3. Read *Matthew 12:33-37* and *James 1:26, 3:1-12*. Where do your words come from? How can you evaluate the health of your heart?

The word for controlling the tongue literally means to bridle. A bridle is a harness used to control a horse by reins with a bit in the mouth. Who is meant to have control over the horse? Who has the reins, the horse or the rider? If James says we are to bridle our tongues in order to bridle our body and lives, then who is supposed to be in control and have the reins?

How can your words measure your state of growth, good or bad?

What about an absence of words from your tongue to God (i.e., a lack of prayer)?

See videos & more under resources at abundantlifestudy.com

- TRANSFORMATION -
ABUNDANT GODLINESS
The New Man Blossoms

—⋘—

But the fruit of the Spirit is love, joy, peace, patience,
kindness, goodness, faithfulness, gentleness and
self-control. Against such things there is no law.
Galatians 5:22-23 NIV

Godliness encompasses a healthy state of reverence, dependence, and devotion to God which results in obedience and displaying Christ-likeness that glorifies God. A Godly person is fulfilling God's purpose for their life by knowing Him in relationship and glorifying Him with their life by displaying His character. They are becoming more like Jesus by spending time with Jesus in His presence and Word. The Abundant Response studied in Part II described one aspect of Godliness, which is our healthy relationship with God. In this lesson we will focus on the manifestations of godliness that change us and are evident to others.

VERSES TO READ, STUDY, AND MEDITATE ON:

1. **Godliness.** These are general verses about Godliness. *1 Timothy 2:1-3, 6:3-12; Titus 1:1-3; 2 Peter 1:1-9, 3:10-13*

2. **Being Conformed to God's Image.** The entire purpose of Christian growth is to make us more like Jesus Christ. The abundant life is a

See videos & more under resources at abundantlifestudy.com

transformation of the heart, mind, and soul to grow closer to God in relationship and to become more like Him in our personage. As this happens you will become more holy because God is holy. Holiness is being set apart to God. Practically, it describes the growth process in which you become more and more "clean" as God "cleans you up" from the "dirt" of sin and the world. *Romans 8:29-30, 12:2; 1 Corinthians 15:49; 2 Corinthians 3:18; Philippians 3:10; Colossians 3:8-11; 1 Peter 1:13-16 (John 3:30)*

3. **Exemplifying God's Character.** The result of being transformed is that you will be more Christ-like in your life and interactions with other people. As the Holy Spirit molds you into the image of Jesus, God's agape love, which is the fruit of the Holy Spirit, will blossom in your life. You will think, act, and speak like the Lord because He is living within you and guiding your life for His purpose and glory. You will love because God is love and has shown you love. You will show grace and mercy because God shows it and because you have received it from Him in abundance (Part I). *Matthew 5:3-12; Luke 6:27-36; John 13:13-17, 15:11-13; 1 Corinthians 11:1; Galatians 5:22-25; Ephesians 5:1-2; Philippians 2:1-11; Colossians 3:12-17; 1 John 2:6 (Micah 6:8; Psalm 112; 2 Timothy 2:24-25; 1 John 4:7-16)*

4. **Glorifying God.** You were created to know God and to glorify Him. You bring Him honor and praise when you obey and love Him with all your heart. The Abundant Results of Part III, where God changes you and you serve God and others, bring Him glory. *Psalm 86:12; Matthew 5:14-16; John 16:13-15, 17:1-5; 1 Corinthians 10:31 (1 Corinthians 6:20, 10:31; 1 Peter 2:11-12, 4:16)*

QUESTIONS TO PONDER:

1. Read *2 Timothy 3:1-5*. What is a form or appearance of Godliness that rejects the power?

Discuss the difference between being outwardly religious and having an inward personal relationship with Jesus Christ. Which is easier?

What signs are listed in these verses to tell you which person you are? Try making a two-column table comparing the characteristics listed in these verses to what they should be if you are truly godly. For example: unloving versus loving, lovers of pleasure versus lovers of God, etc.

2. Read *Galatians 5:22-23*. The fruit is love. The others in the list are aspects of God's agape love. Agape love is unselfish giving. How did Jesus manifest love?

Study the list below:

LOVE (unselfish giving)

JOY (unselfish happiness from God)

PEACE (unselfish harmony with God)

PATIENCE (unselfish waiting)

KINDNESS (unselfish niceness)

GOODNESS (selflessness)

FAITHFULNESS (unselfish dependability)

GENTLENESS/MEEKNESS (unselfish concealed strength under control)

SELF-CONTROL (unselfish revealed strength under control)

Discuss what each of these means and how they all should practically manifest themselves in your life as you mature by the power of the Holy Spirit. Ponder and discuss the selfish counterparts. There is rotten fruit (selfish taking), which is open rebellion (i.e., self-indulgence versus self-control). There is also plastic fruit (selfish giving), which is an imitation of agape love that wants to look real but has underlying selfish motives of giving to get or gain something. Consider how you could selfishly corrupt each aspect of God's love.

See videos & more under resources at abundantlifestudy.com

REFLECTIONS
Week 7

Spend some time in prayer reflecting on this week's lessons. Ask God to speak to your heart and reveal to you what's important. Then spend some time answering the questions below. Write down your responses to discuss them in your small groups or as a journal entry to remember what you have learned.

INSIGHTS:

What are some of the key insights you have learned from this week's lessons? What has stood out to you? What has spoken to your heart?

Lesson 19 • Abundant Growth

Lesson 20 • Abundant Godliness

APPLICATIONS:

How should you respond to what you have learned in this week's lessons? What do you need to do differently? What changes do you feel the Lord leading you to make? What specific steps can you take?

See videos & more
under resources at
abundantlifestudy.com

- TRANSFORMATION -
ABUNDANT STRUGGLE
The New Man Struggles

———≪≪≪≪≪———

For the sinful nature desires what is contrary to the Spirit, and the Spirit what is contrary to the sinful nature. They are in conflict with each other, so that you do not do what you want

Galatians 5:17 NIV

Despite all of the changes and incomprehensible blessings that God has provided for us in His plan of salvation, there are still many struggles and battles that ensue after it has been received. We are fallen because of sin, and so is the world we live in. We have three enemies that will oppose the abundant life by using sin to try to hinder our health and growth. One of them is us! This is called our sinful nature or flesh. Although the sinful nature/flesh is a source of internal battles and struggles, there are two more external enemies to be fought. The other two are the devil/demons and the world. God, however, has provided everything we need to have victory in this life. Our victory will be studied in Lesson 23.

VERSES TO READ, STUDY, AND MEDITATE ON:

1. **The Sinful Nature/Flesh.** The framework of man's existence was corrupted by sin. Not only is the innate person (spirit/soul) corrupted, but also a deeper level of fallen human existence is infected with sin. It is part of your inner being stained with sin that is predisposed to

See videos & more under resources at abundantlifestudy.com

selfishness and sin. This is called "the sinful nature" or "the flesh." The sinful nature/flesh is a source of sinful actions and inner attitudes against God and others.

The sinful nature/flesh remains after salvation. Despite all of the incredible and powerful things God has done to restore mankind from the disease of sin, He has chosen in His infinite wisdom not to rid the Christian of the sinful nature/flesh. Not yet. The cure for this will come in Heaven after physical death. For now, the sinful nature/flesh remains a part of your existence. Do not forget that you have power to prevail! You have God inside you!

This creates within true Christians an internal conflict that must be fought. In your existence you have the Holy Spirit and the sinful nature/flesh living together in the same body. The sinful nature will still be opposed to the things of God and seek selfishness in all areas of life. The new man will desire to know the things of God and do what is right, but the sinful nature/flesh will oppose him. A person who has been saved will begin to struggle with and sometimes overcome sin because he or she now has power over it, something that does not happen before a person is saved. This is actually an important sign of someone who has been genuinely saved by Jesus Christ. Do not be discouraged! *Galatians 5:16-21, 6:7-8; Romans 7:5-25, 8:5-13 (Ephesians 2:1-3; Philippians 3:3-11; Colossians 2:23; 2 Peter 2:10-18)*

OTHER ENEMIES. *A full description of these two additional enemies is beyond the scope of this study, but you need to be aware of their existence and threat to your spiritual health.*

2. **The Devil and Demons.** Evil, demonic forces are real but largely ignored in modern society. A very effective military strategy is for an enemy to make his opponent think he is not a threat or, better yet, that he is not real. The devil and the forces of darkness will attempt to harass, attack, frustrate, and discourage your growth in the Lord. They will also try to deceive you into sinning. *Genesis 3:1-7; Job 1:1-12; John 8:44, 14:30; 2 Corinthians 11:14-15; Luke 4:1-13; 1 John 3:8; 1 Peter 5:8 (Zechariah 3:1-5; 2 Corinthians 4:4, 10:3-6; Ephesians 2:1-3; Revelation 12:9)*

3. **The World.** The "world" is not the physical world of nature but the entire system of fallen human existence that is opposed to the true and living God and His salvation from sin through Jesus Christ. It is ruled by Satan and targets the sinful nature/flesh through lust and pride as means for self-fulfillment and self-preservation. *John 14:30, 15:18-25, 16:33; Romans 12:1-2; 1 John 2:15-17, 3:1, 4:1-3, 5:19; James 1:27, 4:4-6; 2 Peter 1:4 (Mark 4:18-19)*

Holy Spirit + New Man VS. Sinful Nature/Flesh + World + Devil

QUESTIONS TO PONDER:

1. Read *Romans 7:5-25*. This was written by the Apostle Paul about 23 years after he had been saved. Also read *Galatians 5:16-21*. Paul describes the inner battle with the sinful nature/flesh. List two or three things that you struggle with. Have you gained victory over time? Is struggling wrong or a sign of spiritual immaturity? Since the Apostle Paul struggled, then should you get frustrated and view your own struggles as failure? How should you view your struggles?

2. Read and study the following verses: *1 Peter 5:8; 1 John 2:15-17; Romans 12:2; 1 John 5:4-5;* and *John 16:8-11*. Discuss what they teach you about the world, the devil, and their interrelationships.

3. Read *Luke 4:1-13* and *Genesis 3:1-7*. What strategy did Satan use? How does this relate to *1 John 2:15-17*?

See videos & more under resources at abundantlifestudy.com

- TRANSFORMATION -

ABUNDANT SUFFERING

The New Man Suffers

For as we share abundantly in Christ's sufferings, so through Christ we share abundantly in comfort too.

2 Corinthians 1:5 ESV

It is very important for us to understand that the Christian life is not all fun and games. In fact, as we have just learned, it is a war. We live and exist in the middle of a spiritual war in a fallen world ravaged by sin and the enemy. As a result, we will suffer and face great tribulations in this life, but God promises us joy, peace, comfort, and victory to get us through them. Amazingly, He uses them to grow and refine us. Our greatest periods of growth will often come from the most difficult times. If we anticipate suffering and trials and see them as opportunities to grow in the Lord and draw on His power and promises, then half of the victory is won. Perspective is everything. This is part of the renewing of our mind that we studied in Lesson 19.

VERSES TO READ, STUDY, AND MEDITATE ON:

1. **Suffering.** Suffering is when you experience something unpleasant. Something from the outside affects you in a negative way. There are many types of suffering such as physical, financial, emotional, and spiritual. Pain, illness, rejection, and loss can all bring suffering into your life. The Bible is clear that you will suffer as a Christian, but God

See videos & more under resources at abundantlifestudy.com

promises you abundant comfort and even joy in the midst of your suffering. Jesus suffered, and as His disciple, you will too. You can only control your own choices. Choosing to sin brings consequences and its own suffering into your life. This can be prevented by following the Lord. *Luke 9:22; Romans 8:17-25; 2 Corinthians 1:3-7; Philippians 3:10-11; 1 Timothy 4:10; 2 Timothy 3:10-12; Revelation 2:10 (Galatians 6:17; Philippians 1:29-2:2, 4:11-13; Colossians 1:24; 1 Peter 3:13-17)*

2. **Trials and Tribulation.** A trial is a specific event or situation that brings suffering or challenges into your life. There are many types of trials. Some trials you bring upon yourself due to sin and poor decision-making. Other trials come from other people and their sin that affects you. In some situations God orchestrates a trial to test and purify your faith in order to bring you closer to Him and to trust in His provision and power. God is with you in your storms and trials if you turn to Him and trust in Him to get you through them and not necessarily out of them. *John 16:33; Romans 5:3-5; Acts 14:21-22; 1 Peter 1:6-9, 4:12-19; James 1:2-8 (Daniel 3:8-30; Matthew 8:23-27)*

3. **Persecution.** Persecution is another promise that you can expect as a Christian. People will treat you unfairly and seek to harm, ridicule, and restrict your proclamation of Jesus Christ as the Savior of the world. But Christ promises you a special blessing when you suffer for His name's sake! *Matthew 5:10-12, 10:16-31; John 15:18-25; 1 Corinthians 4:11-13; 2 Thessalonians 1:3-5; 2 Timothy 3:10-12*

QUESTIONS TO PONDER:

1. Read *Revelation 2:8-11*. This letter was dictated by Jesus to the church at Smyrna in the first century A.D. What can you learn about suffering and the Christian life from the words of Jesus?

2. What kind of suffering did Jesus endure during his lifetime? What can you expect, based upon your answer and reading of *Luke 17:25, 24:46; and John 15:18-16:4*?

3. In *Philippians 4:18* Paul wrote, "Indeed I have all and abound." Paul claims to be living the abundant life. What is interesting is that Paul is in jail. How could Paul say that? Why did he say it? Discuss Paul's life as a model for the abundant life and the key to enjoying it even in very difficult circumstances.

4. Read *2 Timothy 1:8-12*. Paul also wrote this letter from prison, but this time while on death row. What was Paul focused on that kept him so positive in such difficult circumstances? What can you learn from him? How can you emulate him? Also read *Acts 20:17-24* for insight.

5. Read *Matthew 5:10-12*. Jesus said you are blessed when you are persecuted. Why is this true? How should this truth shape your paradigm of life to enjoy the abundant life?

6. Read *Matthew 13:18-21*. What does this Scripture teach you about the importance of spiritual growth for enduring trials? What was the problem with this person's heart? How can that be corrected? Which type of soil is in your heart?

See videos & more under resources at abundantlifestudy.com

- TRANSFORMATION -
ABUNDANT VICTORY
The New Man Succeeds

⫷⫷⫷⫷

Who shall separate us from the love of Christ? Shall tribulation,
or distress, or persecution, or famine, or nakedness, or peril, or
sword? As it is written: "For Your sake we are killed all day long;
We are accounted as sheep for the slaughter." Yet in all these
things we are more than conquerors through Him who loved us.

Romans 8:35-37 NKJV

We have learned in previous lessons about the many blessings and resources that God has provided for us in Jesus Christ. He provides the means for growth and the power for victory, but He leaves it up to us to tap into this power by choosing to grow, mature, and depend upon Him. If we have a healthy response to God through surrender and relationship, then we will be controlled or "filled" with the Holy Spirit. All of our power for victory comes from God. All of it. Yes, we are a new man with a new heart and mind, but as we have studied, this man is born a baby and must grow, mature, and be renewed by the power of the Holy Spirit as we submit to God and feed on His Word.

We have three strong enemies that are opposing us. We have no chance of victory without surrender, which unleashes God's power and starts our transformation process, enabling us to utilize His power. We have to put on God's armor daily to be ready to fight in the power of His might. Everything that we have learned has

See videos & more
under resources at
abundantlifestudy.com

been building up and combining to make us ready for the victory God has for us. If there is no victory and fruit, then we can trace it back to a lack of relationship and surrender combined with spiritual starvation. Starving Christians simply attending church once a week and praying at meals will have no chance against their flesh, the devil, or the world. In fact, they will resemble the world and cause people not to believe in Jesus Christ because they see no difference between Christians and the world. That is why many Christians are called hypocrites by the world. Christians living the abundant life will not be confused with the world!

VERSES TO READ, STUDY, AND MEDITATE ON:

1. **Walking in the Spirit.** The Word of God talks about "walking in the Spirit" as a means of victory. What does this mean? This is a state where your "walk," or life, is controlled by the Holy Spirit, who is your source of transforming power for victory and change. This comes from being controlled by Him or filled, as you have studied. This reality is absolutely critical. The power switch is turned on when you surrender yourself to God for His will and glory. Abundant health and transformation enable you to walk in the power of the Holy Spirit. This gives you victory over all three of your enemies. (Note: Some translations say "live" instead of "walk.") *Galatians 5:16-26; Romans 8:1-17 (1 John 2:6)*

   Walking in Love. Love is unselfish giving. This means you are to live your life unselfishly. *Ephesians 5:1-2; 2 John 6*

   Walking in the Newness of Life. You are a new creation that has been born again. You should live a new life for God and His glory. *Romans 6:4 (read 6:1-11)*

   Walking in the Light and Truth. Jesus is the way, the truth, and the life. He is the light of the world. He is the Word of God which is a lamp to light your path. *Psalm 119:105; John 8:12; Ephesians 5:8-14; 1 John 1:5-7; 3 John 3-4*

   Walking Circumspectly. You need to live your life carefully and diligently, pursuing the Lord and His will one day at a time. *Ephesians 5:15-17*

Walking by Faith. Biblical faith: God speaks—you hear—you obey. Obeying God is loving God (*John 14:21-24*). If you walk by faith, then you walk in trust, obedience, and love! *2 Corinthians 5:7; Galatians 5:6; Hebrews 11:1-39*

Walking in God's Plan. God has a specific plan for each of us. Walking in His plan is victory. You don't have to know the details in advance, but live by faith the abundant life one day at a time. This is His plan! *Ephesians 2:10*

Walking Worthy. You cannot live a certain way to earn God's love and blessing. Your worthiness comes from Jesus Christ by grace. Through Christ, you can and should, however, live in a way that glorifies God and reflects His worthiness, love, and grace for you. *Ephesians 4:1-5; Philippians 1:27; Colossians 1:9-12 (1 Thessalonians 2:12)*

2. **Victory over Sin.** In Part I you learned about how you have power over sin. This power is a new ability to say no to sin. This power did not exist before you were saved. Because you have died with Christ and have been born again and united with Him, you are dead to sin. You must, however, access the power over sin that God offers you, and you must do this continually to be victorious. You practically begin to walk in this victory when you know what is available to you and then make it real for yourself by presenting yourself to God as His servant who is dead to sin. Review Lesson 8 and the questions you answered on *Romans chapter 6. Focus on verses 3, 6, 11, 13, 16, and 19.*

3. **Victory over the Sinful Nature/Flesh.** The first enemy is you! You studied this notion in Lesson 21. You gain victory over your flesh when you choose to let the Holy Spirit run your life. It should be apparent at this point that everything goes back to surrender, since this unleashes the power of God already in you. If your new man is growing and surrendering, then you will have victory. The Bible talks about "putting off" the deeds of the sinful nature/flesh and "putting on" the new man and Jesus Christ to win victory over sin. This is your role. God has the power and victory ready for you, but you must choose to wear it! You do this by knowing the truth from His Word and then seeking God's power, victory, and will for your life in worship, prayer,

See videos & more under resources at abundantlifestudy.com

surrender, and His Word. This concept directly relates to walking in the Spirit. This spiritual walk will put on Christ and His love and put to death and crucify the sinful nature/flesh, BUT it must be done daily. *Galatians 5:16-26 (Romans 8:1-17)*

Put to death the flesh and put off the old man. *Romans 8:13; Galatians 5:22-25; Ephesians 4:17-32; Colossians 3:5-11*

Put on Christ, the new man, and the armor of God. *Romans 13:11-14; Galatians 3:26-29; Ephesians 4:20-24, 6:10-18; Colossians 3:9-17*

4. **Victory over the Enemy.** God has given you everything you need to be victorious over the enemy. You, however, must activate and use what He has provided through faith and prayer.

    The Armor of God. The armor of God must be understood and put on daily. *Ephesians 6:10-20*

    The Word of God. Jesus defeated the devil by quoting Scripture. The Word of God is the sword of the Spirit. You must know and memorize Scripture to be able to use it when needed. This is having your sword ready. *Ephesians 6:17; Luke 4:1-13; Hebrews 4:12*

    The Presence of God. Staying close to the good Shepherd keeps the wolf (devil) away. If you stray from the Shepherd, then the wolf is more likely to attack. Drawing near to God is a way to resist the devil and provide yourself protection from him. *Psalm 91; John 10:11-16; 15:1-8; Romans 13:11-14; James 4:7-8 (1 Thessalonians 5:8; 1 Peter 5:8-9; 1 John 4:4)*

    The Anointing of God. You have the anointing of the Holy Spirit which gives you spiritual discernment over situations (see Lesson 7). This helps you identify the enemies and their plots against you so that you do not fall for their deceptions and traps. *John 16:13; 1 John 2:20-27 (Philippians 1:9-11)*

The Wisdom of God. You can ask God at any time for wisdom and advice about a situation. What an incredible opportunity! *Proverbs 2:3-22, 3:5-6; James 1:5-8*

The Angels of God. God uses His angels to protect and help you. *Psalm 91:11-13; Daniel 6:22, 10:10-14, 12:1; Hebrews 1:14 (Genesis 19:1-25; Acts 5:19, 12:7)*

The Protection of God. God Himself is your protection and refuge. As a child of God you can call on Him at any time for protection and victory over the enemy. *Psalm 18, 91; Romans 8:31-34; Ephesians 6:18*

The Deliverance of God. God will deliver you from the enemy. *Psalm 34:7, 17, 19; 2 Corinthians 1:9-10; 2 Timothy 3:10-11, 4:17-18 (1 Samuel 26:24; Colossians 1:13)*

The Testimony of God. Your personal testimony is a weapon against the enemy, along with the blood of Jesus Christ which saves you. *Revelation 12:9-11*

The Freedom of God. The enemy is your accuser before God, but you have Jesus Christ as your advocate. He has cleansed you from all your sins and there is no condemnation because you are in Christ. You are free from sin's penalty, power, and condemnation. The devil has nothing to accuse you of before the Father because of Jesus. *Romans 8:1, 33-34; 1 John 2:1*

5. **Victory over the World.** You have already learned that the "world" is not the physical world of nature but the entire system of fallen human existence that is opposed to the true and living God and His salvation from sin through Jesus Christ. It is ruled by Satan and targets the sinful nature/flesh through lust and pride as means for self-fulfillment and self-preservation. You overcome the world by everything that you have studied in this lesson. *John 16:33; 2 Peter 1:3-4; 1 John 5:4-5*

See videos & more
under resources at
abundantlifestudy.com

6. **Victory over Trials and Suffering.** You have already studied trials and suffering in Lesson 22. The most important aspect for victory during life's difficulties is the right perspective. If you remember that God is in control and that He uses trials to help you grow and mature, it changes everything. When you compare your struggles with the coming glory and eternity with the Lord, they begin to shrink and seem less important. God also promises that all things work together for your good even if you do not understand while you are in the middle of your trials. Do not forget, the Lord is with you and comforts you in the midst of it all (see Lesson 22). *Romans 8:18-39; 2 Corinthians 4:17-18; Hebrews 11:24-26 (Acts 20:22-24; John 16:33)*

QUESTIONS TO PONDER:

1. Read *James 4:7-10.* James says to resist the devil and he will flee, but what does James say right before and after this? Why is this integral to resisting the enemy? How do you practically do both?

2. Read *Galatians 5:16-26* and *Romans 8:1-14, 13:11-14.* The key to victory over your flesh is the power of the Holy Spirit. If you can control yourself, then you also gain victory over sin, the devil, and the world because, in the end, you are the culprit. How do you walk in the Spirit? What do you practically need to do to let the Holy Spirit give you the victory? What are the different components of your spiritual life that are necessary for victory? How often does this need to occur?

3. Read *Romans chapter 6*. Go back and focus on *verses 3, 6, 11, 13, 16, and 19.* What are the critical steps you need to take to gain victory over sin?

See videos & more
under resources at
abundantlifestudy.com

REFLECTIONS
Week 8

Spend some time in prayer reflecting on this week's lessons. Ask God to speak to your heart and reveal to you what's important. Then spend some time answering the questions below. Write down your responses to discuss them in your small groups or as a journal entry to remember what you have learned.

INSIGHTS:

What are some of the key insights you have learned from this week's lessons? What has stood out to you? What has spoken to your heart?

Lesson 21 • Abundant Struggle

Lesson 22 • Abundant Suffering

Lesson 23 • Abundant Victory

APPLICATIONS:

How should you respond to what you have learned in this week's lessons?
What do you need to do differently? What changes do you feel the Lord
leading you to make? What specific steps can you take?

- FRUIT -
ABUNDANT LOVE FOR OTHERS
The Focus of Love

—‹‹‹‹‹—

*You did not choose Me, but I chose you and appointed you that
you should go and bear fruit, and that your fruit should remain,
that whatever you ask the Father in My name He may give you.
These things I command you, that you love one another.*
John 15:16-17 NKJV

The abundant transformation that we have just studied results in abundant fruit, which is love. A healthy maturing Christian will be producing the fruit of love in their lives as they are being transformed by God. The heart of love is unselfish giving of ourselves, and the focus of love is others. The Great Commandment is to love God with all of our hearts. This is a given and is essential to health and transformation (Lesson 17). God is first, others are second, and we are last. The only source of love is God. God is agape love. This is why we must be right with God and have His power flowing through us to have any chance of genuinely loving others. Everything must be done in the power of God's love with the other person's best interest at heart. We should love everyone, whether they are believers or unbelievers. We will draw people to Jesus when we love them.

VERSES TO READ, STUDY, AND MEDITATE ON:

1. **Love one another.** God's agape love is the hallmark of being a Christian. Loving one another is the second Great Commandment of God. The

See videos & more
under resources at
abundantlifestudy.com

verses that you will study in #'s 2-17 below are all aspects of love. Love unselfishly gives and cares for others. *Leviticus 19:18; Matthew 22:34-40; John 13:34-35, 15:12-17; Romans 13:8-10; Galatians 5:14, 22-26; James 2:8-9; 1 John 3:23, 4:7-12; 2 John 5 (1 Peter 1:22, 4:8)*

2. **Be devoted to one another.** You are to be devoted to others with a heart ready to help, serve, or minister when needed. *Romans 12:10*

3. **Look out for one another.** You need to look out for the interests of others, whether they are emotional, spiritual, or physical. Your mindset should be concern for their well-being. *Philippians 2:4*

4. **Honor one another.** You should respect one another and see the good in others and their potential to serve God in Christ. *Romans 12:3, 5, 10; 1 Corinthians 12:20-26; Philippians 2:3*

5. **Be honest with one another.** You need honesty to trust other people. Lying and deceiving are of the devil. You will ruin your Christian witness without honesty. *Ephesians 4:25; Colossians 3:9*

6. **Accept one another.** Along with your brothers and sisters in Christ, you are a fallen sinner. Each of us has our own problems and faults. Since God has accepted you, you need to accept each other. *Romans 15:7*

7. **Admonish/instruct one another.** Love warns and even rebukes with the goal of restoration and protection. It is selfish to ignore dangerous or sinful behavior. This must be done in God's timing and can only be accomplished by His love flowing through you. *Romans 15:14; Colossians 3:16*

8. **Agree with one another.** Christians need unity and oneness in Jesus Christ. You will not agree on everything, but you can agree on the essentials of the Gospel, the need to reach the lost, and to love others as yourselves. *Romans 12:16; Philippians 2:2; 1 Corinthians 1:10; 1 Peter 3:8*

9. **Serve and minister to one another.** You need to serve each other and the lost. This will be covered in Lessons 25-27. *Galatians 5:13; 1 Peter 4:10*

10. **Tolerate/bear with one another.** We all have many faults, idiosyncrasies, and weaknesses. Believers need to tolerate and not look down on each other. This does not mean overlooking sin, but it means not expecting everyone else to be perfect or the way you think they should be. The more you realize how fallen you are (a sign of spiritual growth), the more tolerant you will become of others. *Ephesians 4:2; Colossians 3:13*

11. **Forgive one another.** God has forgiven you of all of your sins. You, therefore, must forgive others. Trust is earned but forgiveness is mandatory. *Ephesians 4:32; Colossians 3:13; Mathew 6:14-15; 18:21-35; Luke 23:34*

12. **Be kind and compassionate to one another.** Kindness is unselfish niceness. Compassion empathizes with another person's problems and desires to help that person, leading you to take action on his or her behalf. *Ephesians 4:32; 1 Peter 3:8*

13. **Submit to one another.** You need to humble yourself before God and one another. *Ephesians 5:21-33; 1 Peter 5:5*

14. **Encourage/build up/exhort one another.** You have a great opportunity to encourage others with the Word of God and the Gospel. This is true for the saved and unsaved. God has so many promises and amazing gifts of grace that you could spend the rest of your life encouraging others in the Lord and in His love, grace, and goodness. As you have studied, life is filled with problems and struggles. You can comfort people in their struggles and especially in areas you have already been through due to God's power and grace. *1 Thessalonians 4:18, 5:11; Hebrews 3:13, 10:25*

15. **Motivate one another.** Almost all of us get lazy and need motivation. When I am down, pick me up, and then I will return the favor later. *Hebrews 10:24*

See videos & more under resources at abundantlifestudy.com

16. **Confess to one another.** You should always confess your sins to God, but there are times when you need to confess sins and problems to others for help and guidance or for forgiveness and restoration. *James 5:16*

17. **Pray for one another.** We all need prayer. Pray for each other and for the lost. *1 Thessalonians 5:25; 2 Thessalonians 1:11, 3:1-2; Hebrews 13:18-19 (Colossians 1:9-10)*

QUESTIONS TO PONDER:

1. Read *Philippians 2:1-11*. What does Paul exhort you to do? What is his goal in these verses for you as a Christian? What should the example of Christ encourage and compel you to do?

2. Read *Matthew 18:21-35* and *Ephesians 4:32*. Why must we forgive one another? What happens when you do not forgive but harbor resentment? What is the difference between forgiveness and trust? How do they relate in the forgiveness process?

3. Read *James 5:16* and *1 Thessalonians 5:25*. Why do we need to pray for each other? Read *Luke 6:27-36*. How can praying for someone who has done you wrong help you to love them like the Lord commands? Did God love you when you were His enemy? Read *Romans 5:6-11* and discuss.

See videos & more
under resources at
abundantlifestudy.com

- FRUIT -
ABUNDANT GIVING
The Giving of Love

—‹‹‹‹‹—

But as you abound in everything—in faith, in
speech, in knowledge, in all diligence, and in your
love for us—see that you abound in this grace also.
2 Corinthians 8:7 NKJV

The abundant transformation results in abundant fruit, which is love. God's love can be defined as unselfish, others-centered giving, which is exemplified in its highest form on the cross. God gave His only Son so that we could have eternal life. A growing and maturing Christian will be focused on giving themselves in order to help others in need. This is Christian love in action. Giving makes us more like God, draws us closer to God, enables others to see God, and helps us let go of materialism and our fixation on self.

VERSES TO READ, STUDY, AND MEDITATE ON:

1. **Giving Yourself.** The main thing that you need to give up is yourself! We are naturally self-centered and self-focused in this modern world that we think revolves around us. The power of God in you, however, enables you to give up your time, desires, resources, heart, and life to the will of God. God has given everyone different talents, skills, strengths, testimonies, and resources that can be used to help others for God's glory. It all starts, however, with letting go of yourself.

See videos & more
under resources at
abundantlifestudy.com

Giving Yourself to God. You have already studied in Lesson 12 the essential importance of surrendering your life to God. You must first give yourself back to your Creator for His purpose and glory. Please review Lesson 12 as needed. *Matthew 16:24-27; Mark 10:17-22; Luke 14:25-33; Romans 12:1-2; 2 Corinthians 5:14-15; Revelation 12:11 (Acts 20:24)*

Giving Yourself to Others. Once you have given yourself to God, He will use you to be a blessing to other people. Your heart will naturally have a concern for others and their welfare as the Holy Spirit empowers you to be selfless and focused on others. God gives you your life, talents, and resources to give back to others. You are a channel and conduit for God's blessings to flow to others. *Deuteronomy 15:7-11; Isaiah 58:7-10; 2 Corinthians 8:9-15; Ephesians 5:25, 28-33; 1 Timothy 6:17-19; James 1:27; 1 John 3:16-19 (Romans 16:3-4; Philippians 2:19-30; Hebrews 13:16)*

2. **Giving Your Money.** If God has your heart, then He has your wallet! He does not need your money, but He wants you to invest in His kingdom and in eternal rewards that will last forever. He has chosen to use you to finance His kingdom and ministries. You need to understand that everything you have belongs to the Lord and has been given to you by Him. You are merely giving back what He has first given to you. Giving to God helps your heart be focused on Him, others, and Heaven. It strengthens your faith and blesses you in return! You should give willingly, joyfully, sacrificially, and expectantly. *Genesis 14:17-20, 28:22; Leviticus 27:30; Deuteronomy 14:22-23; Proverbs 3:9-10; Malachi 3:8-11; Matthew 6:19-24; Acts 20:35; 1 Corinthians 16:1-2; 2 Corinthians 8:1-7, 9:6-15; Philippians 4:14-20 (Genesis 28:22; Proverbs 11:25, 22:9; Matthew 23:23; Luke 6:38)*

QUESTIONS TO PONDER:

1. Read *Matthew 6:19-21.* What are the "treasures" on earth that will rot, decay, and be stolen? What are the "treasures" in Heaven that are immune to this? What is the difference? Why? How do we lay up treasures in Heaven?

What does it mean that where your treasure is your heart will follow?

How can you use this principle to draw closer to God and His purposes?

2. Read *1 John 3:16-19*. What should you do for a brother/sister in need? How do you do that practically? Should you take the credit as a "good person" or give the credit and glory to God? What is the blessing that you get for helping others?

See videos & more under resources at abundantlifestudy.com

REFLECTIONS
Week 9

Spend some time in prayer reflecting on this week's lessons. Ask God to speak to your heart and reveal to you what's important. Then spend some time answering the questions below. Write down your responses to discuss them in your small groups or as a journal entry to remember what you have learned.

INSIGHTS:

What are some of the key insights you have learned from this week's lessons? What has stood out to you? What has spoken to your heart?

Lesson 24 • Abundant Love for Others

Lesson 25 • Abundant Giving

REFLECTIONS

WEEK 9

APPLICATIONS:

How should you respond to what you have learned in this week's lessons?
What do you need to do differently? What changes do you feel the Lord
leading you to make? What specific steps can you take?

See videos & more
under resources at
abundantlifestudy.com

- FRUIT -
ABUNDANT SERVICE
The Servant of Love

—‹‹‹‹‹—

Whoever desires to become great among you shall be your
servant. And whoever of you desires to be first shall be slave
of all. For even the Son of Man did not come to be served, but
to serve, and to give His life a ransom for many.
Mark 10:43-45 NKJV

The Lord Jesus Christ was the perfect servant while He was on earth. His entire life and ministry was about others. He never did anything to benefit Himself. He never used His power to help Himself. He came to die so that others might live through Him. As Christians, we are to follow His example and give up our lives to serve God and others. When we serve God, He has us serve others. When we serve others, we are serving God.

There are many ways and places to be a servant. We should serve at home, at church, in the workplace, and in the world. We should serve God, our families, fellow Christians, friends, neighbors, and the world around us. The power to be a servant comes from God living within us. The perfect servant, Jesus Christ, lives within us and can empower us to glorify Him if we surrender to His will and abide in His power, presence, and Word to do it. We must avoid serving ourselves at the expense of others.

See videos & more
under resources at
abundantlifestudy.com

VERSES TO READ, STUDY, AND MEDITATE ON:

1. **Serving God.** In Lesson 12 you studied how you are a bondservant. You should view yourself as God's servant, created to glorify Him and serve others. There are many ways that you can serve God, and you have already reviewed many of them in other lessons. If you are surrendered to the Lord and walking in His will by the power of the Holy Spirit, then you will naturally be serving God and others, which brings Him glory. The essential ingredient is surrender, because you must be doing the will of God in your service to Him. Serving God is serving others since God is all about other people. Jesus is our example of the perfect servant. *Matthew 24:45-51; 1 Corinthians 15:58; Colossians 3:22-24; 2 Timothy 2:3-4 (Philippians 2:5-11; 1 Thessalonians 1:9)*

2. **Serving Others.** You can serve others in the name of the Lord in many ways. You can help people, pray for them, encourage them, be with them in hard times, teach them, and support them, just to name a few. God wants His people to serve each other and to serve the unbelieving world as a way of demonstrating the love of God to them. You should be serving others everywhere you go—home, school, work, church, the world, etc. Being a servant makes other people and their welfare your priority. All of the "one anothers" we studied in the last lesson are forms of serving others. *Mark 9:33-35, 10:43-45; John 13:1-17; 1 Corinthians 9:19-23; Galatians 5:13-15, 6:2; Philippians 2:1-4; 2 Timothy 2:24-26*

QUESTIONS TO PONDER:

1. Read *Colossians 1:3-8, 4:7-9*, and *Philippians 2:19-30*. What can you learn about being a servant from these descriptions of Epaphras, Tychicus, Timothy, and Epaphroditus?

2. Since Jesus is the perfect servant, what can you learn about being a servant to God and others from the life of Christ? List at least eight characteristics of the Lord that you should strive to emulate in serving. Give specific Scripture references if you can.

3. What are the lives of servants like? What kind of daily life do they have? How do they view their lives? What would they do when they first start their day? What do they own? Explore the life of a servant and how this can help you to be a better servant of God and others.

See videos & more under resources at abundantlifestudy.com

- FRUIT -
ABUNDANT HARVEST
The Goal of Love

————≪≪≪≪————

*The harvest truly is plentiful, but the laborers
are few. Therefore pray the Lord of the
harvest to send out laborers into His harvest.*
Matthew 9:37-38 NKJV

The ultimate goal of God is to save people. Jesus Christ came to save sinners by dying on the cross for the sins of the world. Our goal should be to win people to Christ. We should see every person as God's creation that He loves, died for, and cares about more than we can ever comprehend. As we grow and mature in the Lord, we should begin to share our faith and have a heart for the lost. Our relationship with God which keeps discovering the depths of His love should compel us to try to reach the lost. We are only responsible for presenting the Gospel in a loving and appropriate way. Anyone can give their testimony. We cannot save anyone or convince anyone to be a Christian. It is up to God to save them and up to the person to choose Christ.

VERSES TO READ, STUDY, AND MEDITATE ON:

1. **Ambassadors of the Gospel.** God has declared that you are His ambassador of the Gospel. You are His representative who has been entrusted to tell everyone what He has done on the cross. He has given you the ministry of reconciliation. He wants you to plead His case of love to a lost and dying world. *2 Corinthians 5:18-21*

See videos & more
under resources at
abundantlifestudy.com

2. **Spreading the Gospel.** You have been given the greatest message with the greatest story of all time. God has entrusted it to you and commanded you to tell as many people as you can. *Matthew 28:18-20; Mark 16:15; John 15:27, 20:21; Acts 1:8, 4:33; 1 John 4:14 (Luke 14:15-24, 24:46-49; Acts 5:32; 1 Corinthians 1:17; Philemon 6)*

3. **Sowing and Watering the Gospel.** God has given you an analogy for spreading His word of salvation: It is like planting a seed. A seed must be planted in fertile soil and be watered. You can plant seeds in people's hearts and water them by telling them about Jesus and then showing them His love in your service and kindness to them. You plant seeds by loving people and serving them. When you share the Good News of Jesus with people, you have no idea who has planted and watered before you. It could be harvest time! The seeds will later germinate and give you an opportunity to directly share the reason for your caring about them. People need to know that you care before they will listen to what you believe. *Luke 8:4-15; John 4:34-38; 1 Corinthians 3:5-8*

4. **Not Ashamed of the Gospel.** Sometimes Christians can be ashamed or embarrassed to tell people about Christ. You might worry about what they will think and fear their rejection, but you should not be ashamed or afraid. You have the power of God in your message and living within you. The more you have the love of God in your heart from devotion and worship, the easier it will be to share your faith. You will be compelled to tell people because it is bursting out of you. You cannot judge your effectiveness by their response. *Romans 1:16; 2 Timothy 1:8-12; 1 Corinthians 1:18; Psalm 40:9-10, 71:14-16, 119:46; Mark 8:38*

5. **A Heart for the Gospel and the Lost.** God has a heart for the Gospel and the lost, and so should you. If you are in a right relationship with the Lord, then you should have a burden to tell people about His salvation. You should fear for their souls and desire that they experience not only salvation, but the loving relationship that you have right now. Your selfish, sinful nature will not care, but the Holy Spirit living within you can give you this desire and heart for the lost that comes from God. The reality of God living within you and your state of eternal life now is also a stark reminder of the reality of the separation from God to those all around and warns them of the danger of entering eternity

without God. *Psalm 119:136; Isaiah 6:8; Luke 19:10; Romans 9:1-3, 10:1; 1 Corinthians 9:19-23, 10:33; 2 Corinthians 5:14-16; 2 Timothy 2:8-10, 4:1-5 (1 Corinthians 2:1-5)*

6. **Ready to Share the Gospel.** You need to be ready to share the Gospel. How can you be ready? You can rehearse your testimony, pray for God to enable you to share in a loving way, and have a Bible or tracts on hand in case a situation arises in your path. You also need to be waiting, watching, and expecting God to give you divine appointments to share your faith or begin to build relationships that will one day enable you to share. You need to walk with a God-consciousness and be tuned in to the fact that even in the midst of your busy life He is about saving souls. He gave His life! He is eager for you to tell people what He has done for them. You can also read books, study, and make sure you know basic Bible verses about salvation like *John 3:16, Romans 3:23, 6:23*, and *10:8-10*. If you are praying and watching, then God will give you an open "door" to tell someone about Jesus Christ. *Romans 1:15; 1 Corinthians 16:9; 2 Corinthians 2:12; Colossians 4:2-5; 2 Timothy 4:1-5; 1 Peter 3:15-16*

QUESTIONS TO PONDER:

1. Read *John 4:1-42*. What can you learn about witnessing from Jesus and His interaction with the woman at the well? How does He start the conversation? How does He change the topic to the spiritual realm? How does He deal with the woman's sin?

See videos & more under resources at abundantlifestudy.com

2. Read *Luke 8:4-15*. What is the seed? What is the ground that the seed falls on? What can you learn from this parable about how people will respond to the salvation message? Did the sower selectively spread his seed? If you sense there is a problem with the soil/ground, what can you do to change it? Who has that power?

3. Read *2 Corinthians 5:18-21*. What is an ambassador? What can you learn from the role of an ambassador about your responsibility to share the Gospel with the lost?

4. Read *Acts 22:1-21* and *26:1-32*. What can you learn from the Apostle Paul giving his testimony? What does he appeal to? What is his strategy? How does he ask for a response?

See videos & more
under resources at
abundantlifestudy.com

REFLECTIONS
Week 10

Spend some time in prayer reflecting on this week's lessons. Ask God to speak to your heart and reveal to you what's important. Then spend some time answering the questions below. Write down your responses to discuss them in your small groups or as a journal entry to remember what you have learned.

INSIGHTS:

What are some of the key insights you have learned from this week's lessons? What has stood out to you? What has spoken to your heart?

Lesson 26 • Abundant Service

Lesson 27 • Abundant Harvest

APPLICATIONS:

How should you respond to what you have learned in this week's lessons? What do you need to do differently? What changes do you feel the Lord leading you to make? What specific steps can you take?

See videos & more
under resources at
abundantlifestudy.com

201

THE ABUNDANT LIFE PATHWAY

- REVIEW -

The figure on the next page summarizes The Abundant Life pathway. It all starts with abundant revelation from the Word of God. This revelation of the grace of God is so amazing and incredible that the believer then has an abundant response to God that is initiated through surrender. The abundant response of the believer to God's revelation results in God responding back. This sets up a feedback loop creating an abundant relationship, which defines the abundant state of spiritual health. The abundant results are the natural outflow and result of abundant health. All of these feed back into each other, creating a continuing cycle of increasing spiritual growth, health, and results.

The more we learn about our Heavenly Father and Lord Jesus Christ, the more we respond and grow in Him, which opens up more room for the cycle to continue. We fall deeper and deeper in love and are increasingly amazed at the Person and work of God in our lives. The more we grow and know, the more we surrender and serve from gratitude, awe, and wonder.

PART I

ABUNDANT REVELATION

PART II

ABUNDANT RESPONSE

ABUNDANT HEALTH

PART III

ABUNDANT RESULTS

See videos & more
under resources at
abundantlifestudy.com

OTHER WORKS
OTHER RESOURCES BY DR. GREG VIEHMAN

THE GOD DIAGNOSIS

A SUCCESSFUL PHYSICIAN MAKES THE MOST STARTLING AND UNEXPECTED DIAGNOSIS OF HIS LIFE.

Unsettled by the mysteries of purpose and destiny, Dr. Viehman takes the reader on an emotionally palpable and transforming journey through cynicism, skepticism and discovery. The God Diagnosis is a detailed and compelling testimony of a skilled surgeon who himself undergoes a "heart transplant."

www.goddiagnosis.com

You can purchase 'The God Diagnosis' at these digital locations:

Also available in multiple languages.

EVERLAS✝ING STRENGTH

www.everlastingstrength.org

Everlasting Strength seeks to demonstrate the love of Jesus Christ by evangelism, biblical teaching, and charitable giving so that people may know God in a growing, personal, and saving relationship that increasingly glorifies Him with their lives. Visit Everlasting Strength to sign up for Dr. Viehman's blog, view his testimony and select speaking engagements, and interact with other biblical resources to grow in the Lord and be on fire for the Gospel! The Lord and His Word are awesome and something to be excited about!

www.everlastingstrength.org